Physical Characteristics of the Briard

(from the American Kennel Club breed standard)

Topline: The Briard is constructed with a very slight incline, downward from the prominent withers to the back which is straight, to the broad loin and the croup which is slightly inclined. The croup is well muscled and slightly sloped to give a well-rounded finish. The topline is strong, never swayed nor roached.

Body: Chest is broad and deep with moderately curved ribs, egg-shaped in form, the ribs not too rounded. The breastbone is moderately advanced in front, descending smoothly to the level of the elbows and shaped to give good depth to the chest.

Hindquarters: Powerful, providing flexible, almost tireless movement. Two dewclaws are required on each rear leg, placed low on the leg, giving a wide base to the foot.

Tail: Uncut, well feathered, forming a crook at the extremity, carried low and not deviating to the right or to the left.

Coat: The outer coat is coarse, hard and dry. It lies down flat, falling naturally in long, slightly waving locks. The undercoat is fine and tight on all the body.

Color: All uniform colors are permitted except white.

Feet: Strong and rounded, being slightly oval in shape. The toes are strong, well arched and compact.

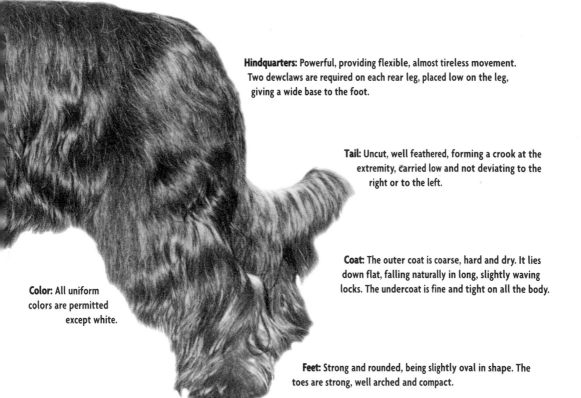

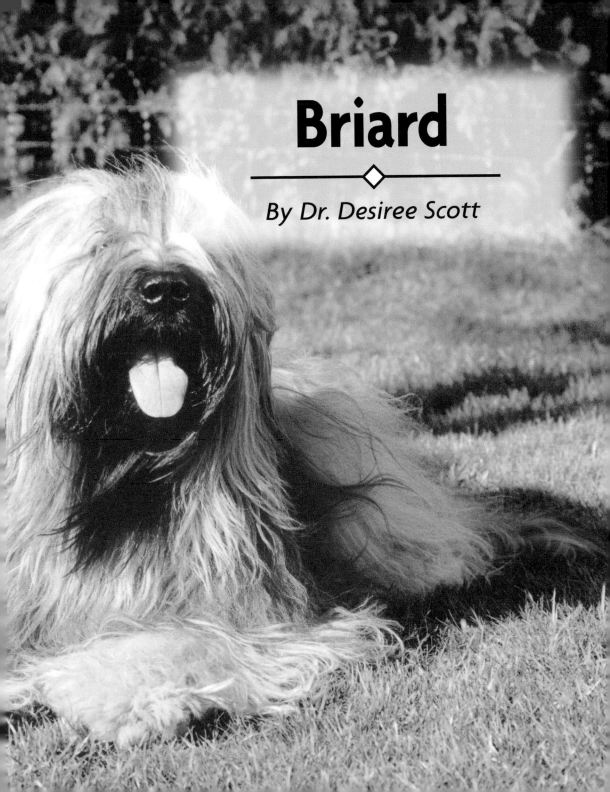

Briard

By Dr. Desiree Scott

Contents

9

History of the Briard

Trace the origins of the European livestock guardians from their earliest domestication to the spread of these working sheepdogs through Europe and Asia. Visit 19th-century France to meet the early Briards, and travel with these dogs through history to modern-day Britain, the US and beyond.

23

Characteristics of the Briard

Is the Briard right for you? Find out about the breed's personality, requirements and virtues, including the breed's health considerations, special abilities and color possibilities, described by the author in terms of the breed's genetics. Discuss concerns about what every owner should know before purchasing a puppy.

36

Breed Standard for the Briard

Learn the requirements of a well-bred Briard by studying the description of the breed set forth in the American Kennel Club standard. Both show dogs and pets must possess key characteristics as outlined in the breed standard.

52

Your Puppy Briard

Find out about how to locate a well-bred Briard puppy. Discover which questions to ask the breeder and what to expect when visiting the litter. Prepare for your puppy-accessory shopping spree. Also discussed are home safety, the first trip to the vet, socialization and solving basic puppy problems.

74

Proper Care of Your Briard

Cover the specifics of taking care of your Briard every day: feeding for the puppy, adult and senior dog; grooming, including coat care, ears, eyes, nails and bathing; and exercise needs for your dog. Also discussed are the essentials of dog identification.

Training Your Briard 90

Begin with the basics of training the puppy and adult dog. Learn the principles of house-training the Briard, including the use of crates and basic scent instincts. Enter puppy kindergarten and introduce the pup to his collar and leash and progress to the basic commands. Find out about obedience classes and other activities.

Healthcare of Your Briard 111

By Lowell Ackerman DVM, DACVD
Become your dog's healthcare advocate and a well-educated canine keeper. Select a skilled and able veterinarian. Discuss pet insurance, vaccinations and infectious diseases, the neuter/spay decision and a sensible, effective plan for parasite control, including fleas, ticks and worms.

Your Senior Briard 140

Know when to consider your Briard a senior and what special needs he will have. Learn to recognize the signs of aging in terms of physical and behavioral traits and what your vet can do to optimize your dog's golden years.

Showing Your Briard 144

Step into the center ring and find out about the world of showing pure-bred dogs. Here's how to get started in AKC shows, how they are organized and what's required for your dog to become a champion. Take a leap into the realms of obedience trials, agility trials and competitive herding events.

Index 156

KENNEL CLUB BOOKS® **BRIARD**
ISBN: 1-59378-295-0

Copyright © 2006 • Kennel Club Books, LLC
308 Main Street, Allenhurst, NJ 07711 USA
Cover Design Patented: US 6,435,559 B2 • Printed in South Korea

Photography by Isabelle Français, Carol Ann Johnson, Dr. Desiree Scott and Michael Trafford
with additional photographs by:

Paulette Braun, Alan and Sandy Carey, Carolina Biological Supply, Juli (Moss) Carralejo, Katri and Markku Espo, Bill Jonas, Dr. Dennis Kunkel, M. Marks, Tam C. Nguyen, Phototake, Jamie Putnam, Jean Claude Revy, Stewart Event Images, Chuck Tatham, Alice van Kempen and Mary Weir-Anderson.

Illustrations by Dr. Desiree Scott.

The publisher wishes to thank all of the owners whose dogs are illustrated in this book.

Ch. Déjà Vu Woodbine Cheap Thrills, Ch. Déjà Vu Four Leaf Clover and Ch. C'est Bonheur Woodbine Tinsel.

HISTORY OF THE

BRIARD

The Briard is one of a large group of European sheepdogs characterized by the hair on their chins, which forms beards. Briards come from France, and their hairy relatives stretch from the Balkans to Scotland.

The Briard is a sheepdog that descends from an ancient type of dog called the livestock guardian. Livestock guardians work with sheep in a protective way; the Briard and its smooth-coated relation, the Beauceron, are more recent types that can be used to move sheep as well as guard them.

Notice that I do not use the word "breed" when referring to dogs of long ago. There was no such thing as a breed of dog until the mid-19th century, when the Victorians invented dog shows and the differently shaped dogs were formally classified for the first time. Until this time, there were only different dog types.

DOMESTICATION AND CLASSIFICATION

There is no way of knowing exactly when or how domestication came about, but this easier way of life must certainly have been appreciated by wolves and their kin. Our dogs are provided with food, shelter,

THE STORY OF THE CHIEN D'AUBREY

There are several romantic stories concerning how the Briard got its name. It is not connected in a specific way to the French area of Brie (from where the cheese comes), and it has been said that "Briard" is a corruption of the name "Chien d'Aubrey." Sir Aubrey de Montdidier was a French aristocrat who was murdered in 1371 in front of his dog. Every time the dog came across the assassin, the dog became enraged and tried to attack the killer. The King of France ordered that a duel should take place between the dog and the accused, a man named Richard de Macaire. The dog was the victor, and Macaire confessed and was beheaded.

medical care and many other extras. In the past, human support was not as comprehensive as that which the modern pet now receives, but the garbage dumps of the first human settlements were easy places for dogs to rifle for scraps. Those dogs that were the least afraid of people fared the best, for it was a real waste of energy to run away all the time.

Furthermore, if the dogs could have their puppies near these dumps, which were the food sources, they conserved the energy that would have been used by trailing back to the den with food. Once the more sentimental members of the human communi-

ties saw the puppies, people started to have a direct effect on domestication by giving extra protection to the most people-friendly puppies.

Once sheep were domesticated, selection pressure was put on the village dogs, thus separating them into the two earliest dog types: the sheep-friendly livestock guardians and the sighthounds, which retained their adult killing behavior patterns.

The earliest dog breeders did not choose their dogs because of their appearance but because of their behavior patterns. The reason that livestock guardians are safe with domestic livestock is that they retain the behavior patterns of puppies and remain at the "play" stage all their lives. They retain the juvenile physical traits of floppy ears, big heads and facial wrinkles that the sighthound puppy soon outgrows.

The dogs that were not livestock guardians, the ones that were not livestock-friendly because they displayed their full adult behavior patterns, were retained because of their hunting prowess; these were the sighthounds.

SPREAD OF THE LIVESTOCK GUARDIANS

The livestock guardians and the sighthounds first developed in the area where farming and the domestication of sheep originated. Recent DNA analysis on domesticated wheat have traced this back to

Even in our modern society, Briards still perform in their bred-for capacities: guarding livestock, property and family.

the southeastern border of Turkey, next to Iraq. It is from this area that both of these types of dog spread, with other domesticated animals (goats and cattle), both east and west. Going east, they arrived in Tibet and China, which is exactly the reverse of what most dog books say. The books do not give any explanation of how a farming dog spontaneously appeared in an area where agriculture came much later. The Tibetan Mastiff is the livestock guardian of the Himalayas, but it is derived from the dogs of the Near East—how could it be the ancestor of dogs developed in Turkey many hundreds of years before?

France, however, is in the opposite direction of Tibet, and we have to follow the spread of farming into Europe from the Near East during the Neolithic, or New Stone, Age. The reason that archaeologists gave names such as "Stone Age" and "Iron Age" is that when serious studies of these eras began, there were no techniques with which to work out exact dates; thus, the period of time before metal implements were used was called the Stone Age. Even so, the axes and other tools made from stone were highly polished to make sharp blades and were very effective. The main problem with them was that they could not last as long as the metal tools that were to follow.

Dogs from Turkey. On the right is a Saluki-type sighthound. The dog on the left is the livestock guardian type that we know as an Anatolian Shepherd Dog.

Although shepherding is not as popular in the 21st century as it was in past centuries, the Briard still serves in this capacity for European farmers.

The actual date of the Neolithic Age varies from place to place, for the change to farming occurred in the Near East before moving through Turkey into the Balkans and Greece, then along the rivers of Europe to the Atlantic coast of France by about 5500–4700 BC, crossing into Britain sometime after 4500 BC.

We can plot livestock guardians across Europe. The first places that were farmed were those that had the best soil—the areas next to rivers—and the last areas to be farmed were the poor soils of mountains. However, since that time farming techniques have advanced in the lowland areas, and it is now only in the mountains that the old ways of looking after sheep are still used. This means that many of the remnant populations of livestock guardians are found in mountain ranges, and are called "Mountain Dogs" by us. Examples of these livestock guardians are the Great Pyrenees (called the Pyrenean Mountain Dog outside the US), the Estrela Mountain Dog of Portugal and the Bernese Mountain Dog.

If we look at the map showing how farming spread, we can see how the major rivers were important in spreading this way of life. And if we look at the livestock guardians of Greece, Romania and the former Yugoslavia, we see a close similarity. These dogs are almost unchanged from their original form because there is only a very short history of dog shows in these countries. With the coming of dog-show competition, dog breeders have altered the appearance of many breeds to make them more "glamorous."

The spread of farming into Europe. The yellow areas are those where the first farmers lived.

The bearded Komondor comes from Hungary and is known for its white corded coat and great size.

THE BEARDED SHEEPDOGS

Long-distance trading took place long before the first use of metals, and one of the areas in which the greatest markets took place was the Carpathian Basin, an area that is now part of Hungary and Romania. If we plot the geographical origin of all of today's livestock guardians, we find a new type of dog appearing here—the livestock guardian with a beard. In Hungary it is the Komondor and in Romania the very similar Mioritic Sheepdog, with the

The smooth-coated relative of the Briard, the Beauceron is gaining recognition around the world as a competent guard dog and protector.

South Russian Ovcharka found in the southeastern republics that used to be part of the Soviet Union.

The "bearded" sheepdogs extended over Europe to the Bearded Collie of Scotland and to the east to the Kyi Apso of Tibet. The Kyi Apso is similar to the Tibetan Mastiff, with a coat like that of a scruffy Lhasa Apso.

SHEEPDOGS OF FRANCE

France has many native breeds, and among these are five sheepdog breeds that are internationally recognized. There are a number of unrecognized types from the South of France as well, but these are not as yet being selectively bred. The Picardy Sheepdog belongs to the German/Belgian/Dutch Shepherd Dog complex, but the others are more closely related to each other.

The Briard is the large hairy French sheepdog, while the Beauceron is the smooth version. The Pyrenean Sheepdog is the small hairy type, with the Smooth-faced Pyrenean Sheepdog less hairy, but not completely smooth-coated.

When the first dog show was held in Paris in 1863, there were a dozen French sheepdogs entered, all of diverse shapes and sizes. The most numerous were dogs of a smooth-haired breed, black and tan in color—the breed that is now known as the Beauceron. There were also two representatives of the hairy sheepdog known as the Briard. The first Briard was registered in the

French Stud Book in 1885, and the first Beauceron in 1893. The Beauceron and the Briard were not officially separated until 1896. The Picardy Sheepdog only received recognition in 1922, and the Pyrenean Sheepdog in 1926.

The complex matter of the Briard's color can only be understood by considering its shared origin with the black and tan Beauceron. This is why bicolor is unacceptable in the Briard, as it demonstrated a Beauceron too near in the pedigree at the time when the two breeds were regularly crossed.

EFFECTS OF WAR ON THE BRIARD

Once World War I began, the Briard found another job working at the French front line. When the United States joined this war near its

Male and female Pyrenean Sheepdogs with a puppy. As companions, these are delightful, happy dogs to share one's life with.

conclusion the American soldiers were able to see this large dog in action. They must have been impressed, for the breed was taken back to the United States, with the first American-bred litter being born in 1922. In 1931, the black import Regent de la Pommeraie became the first American champion. Interestingly, the first American-bred

MADEMOISELLE TURGIS

The first winner of a British Challenge Certificate was the French import Desamee Tripot de Vasouy, bred by Mademoiselle Turgis in her chateau in Honfleur, Normandy. Apparently the chateau was filled with priceless antiques as well as Briards of a special rich hue of fawn. During the German occupation of France in the 1940s, she worked for the French resistance, hiding British servicemen on her estate. This was a fairly safe place to be, as the Germans were afraid of the Briards that roamed around her walled garden. On the rare occasions that they came to search the chateau, Mme. Turgis would call out the names of dogs, using fictitious names so that the servicemen would know to climb out the window and hide in the woods.

Her mode of transport was a cart pulled by two Briards, and with this she smuggled the extra food rations she needed for her secret guests. It was generally a successful mode of transport; however, on one occasion a young Briard saw a cat in a shop window and started to chase it, bringing the cart, its owner and the other Briard with him. The servicemen did manage to get back to England and, as a gesture of thanks after the war, their officer gave Mme. Turgis a little car.

A WORD ABOUT DOG SHOWS

In Europe, the emphasis for dog breeders is slightly different from what it is in Britain and the United States. As well as placing the dogs at shows, the judge also grades the dog on how typical it is of the breed, with the top grade being Excellent. All of the prizewinners have to be graded Excellent; if no dog of this quality is present, then no prizes are awarded.

The largest show for one breed in the world is the annual German Sieger show for the German Shepherd Dog, where there is an entry of 2000 or so dogs. In the class for adult males, there are more than 150 dogs entered and every dog is graded, even if it comes in last place. Out of these, only ten or so are graded Excellent; thus, going home with a grade of Excellent from a show like this is an award of great importance—much more so than the group placements that some American and British people chase after, and where only first over any other dog will do.

The French Briard equivalent of the Seiger show is the Rassemblement, and this was first held in 1970. In 1983, 900 Briards were entered, with 11 dogs and 11 bitches graded Excellent. Again, all of the entries are evaluated, and temperament and working ability are considered as well as conformation. The Briard Club of America holds a North American Rassemblement every four years, producing a book with photos of each dog, along with its pedigree and the point-by point-evaluation, the most wonderful source of information for choosing Briard parents.

champion was described as black with tan markings.

There had been a French breed club set up just before World War I, but with the German invasion in 1914 such activities were stopped. The club was reformed in 1924, but the whole of France had to undergo an even more horrific occupation in 1940 when the Nazis invaded. This almost destroyed every facet of French life. There was a puppet government set up by the Germans, but many French fled to Britain to plan for liberation of their country, leaving those who formed the resistance to hide their activities as best they could. There was little time for breeding dogs; there was even less time for the keeping of accurate pedigrees.

The Briard survived the war in a much healthier state than the Beauceron, but many were requisitioned as army guard dogs. The Beauceron gene pool was greatly depleted, and faults that had not been problems before the war occurred—pale eyes, missing teeth and lack of conformation and type. Popularity had shifted, and the Briard was now much more numerous than the smooth-haired Beauceron.

THE BRIARD COMES TO BRITAIN

The Briard came to Britain in 1966 when Nancy Tomlin went to Ireland to join her husband Mike, who was working with a film crew. They had been thinking of a puppy, and the idea of an Irish Wolfhound appealed to them. They went to visit a large multiple-breed kennel called Shannon kennels, which had been set up by an American wishing to export to the American market. Though this was a commercial set-up, the foundation stock that had been chosen was of good quality. Indeed, when the kennel folded in 1968, many of the Briards there found their way to Britain and are behind the British show population.

During the visit to Shannon kennels in 1966, Mrs. Tomlin fell in love with a bouncy black four-month-old Briard called Hubert and brought him home to London. Soon the British canine press, and the general press as well, had pictures of this black hairy dog, the likes of which had never been seen before. He was soon joined at the Tomlins

From the turn of the 20th century, this is how the Briard looked around 1900.

by his half-sister Maudie. Soon Mr. and Mrs. Trueman, who ran the local training classes, had Briards too; they even had Maudie's parents brought over from Ireland.

The Tomlins registered their kennel name as Desamee, and Desamee Leon Hubert and Desamee Mitzi Moffat (Maudie) were gracing the show ring. The first show that had classes for the Briard was in 1970, but things moved quickly, and by 1974 there were classes at Crufts with Challenge Certificates (CCs) available. Winning three of these CCs gains a dog the title of Champion in Britain, and the first Briard to do this was Maudie herself. Sadly, she died later in 1974 after a Caesarean operation. The winner of the Challenge Certificate for best dog that year at Crufts was a fawn French import, Desamee Tripot de Vasouy, who had to wait until Crufts in 1976 to win his champion title. CCs were only offered at 6 shows each year at that time, but by 2000 there would be 21 pairs of CCs awarded.

Eng. Ch. Desamee Tripot de Vasouy, a French import who became a champion in the UK.

Ch. Panthere del Pastre, imported from France, owner-handled by R. Tingley to BIS at Woodstock Dog Club in 1982 under judge R. Turton. Panthere won the Briard Club of America national specialty in 1983 and also placed in the Group at Westminster.

WOODSTOCK DOG CLUB
BEST IN SHOW

THE ARRIVAL OF THE BRIARD IN THE UNITED STATES

The first Briard to be registered by the American Kennel Club was Dauphine de Montjoye, whose name was inscribed in the Stud Book in June 1928. She was born in France, bred by Mademoiselle Raoul Duval and imported by Miss Frances Hoppin of Cornwall on Hudson, New York, who was one of the founder members of the Briard Club of America. Interestingly, Dauphine's color was described as black and tan.

In 1931 French import Ch. Regent de la Pommeraie became the first American champion. He was black and owned by Mrs. Albert Whelan at the time of his title.

The Briard had a low profile as a show dog in the era before World War II. Some very wealthy exhibitors were importing dogs from breeds that had been specially selected for the show ring for decades, and the more "homespun"-looking Briard was defeated by the

Rough Collies of Mrs. Florence B. Ilch's Bellhaven kennel, Mrs. Geraldine Rockefeller Dodge's German Shepherds and Doberman Pinschers, not to mention at the Best in Show level by the Fox and Airedale Terriers that were winning titles in Britain and the States at a time when the only way of Atlantic travcling was by the great sea-going liners. The Herding Group was only created in 1982, so competition at this time for the Briard was in the Working Group—that is how a Briard could be defeated by a Doberman in this competition.

In 1956 Irene Castle Khatoonian Schlintz published her Phillips System of Top Dogs, the first attempt anywhere in the world to calculate the top-winning dogs of all breeds in any one country.

During the first decade no Briard was among the top ten of all working dogs, and Boxers had joined the Dobermans as the top-scoring breeds. A dog's Phillips score starts when he wins a Group placement, and the first Briard to collect these points was Ch. Niobe Chez Phydeaux in 1966; indeed he was the only Group-placing Briard that year.

In 1970 an import from France, Ch. Nanie de la Haute Tour, won a Working Group, but she was not top Briard, as her son Ch. Phydeaux Quoin de Cuivre's 12 placements of Group Four meant that he had defeated many more dogs than she had. He was still top Briard in 1974

because of his multiple Group placements, as Group One (first place) still eluded him, but two other Nanie children, his litter brother Ch. Phydeaux Quelques and Ch. Pythias Chez Phydeaux, each won a Group that year.

The first multiple Group winner was Ch. Stonehills I'm Henri, who won five in 1975; following this was another seven in 1976, plus another seven in 1977.

The first Best in Show winner from 1956 on (and here is a job for Briard historians—any BIS wins 1928–1955?) was French import Ch. Jennie d'el Pastre, whose 4 BIS wins, 17 Groups and 33 Group placements, all in 1978, made her the fifth best working dog of all breeds that year. The Briard was now making its mark in all-breed competition; the standard of presen-tation was such that a coat that was not in the finest bloom was marked down, and the benefit of adding top-class French imports to the breeding

Ch. Phydeaux Polly Poulet, BIS at Holland, Michigan KC in 1983 under judge Kurt Mueller.

Ch. Beardsanbrow's Utopia, a two-time national specialty (1989 and 1991) winner, a multiple BIS winner in Canada and a top sire, shown by Woody Wornall to a Group win at Santa Barbara KC.

pool was being felt. Ch. Phydeaux What's Happening was fourth of all the breeds in the still large Working Group in 1980, with 5 BIS, 22 Groups and 35 Group placements that year. He was a grandson of Nanie through Quoin de Cuivre, and one of his Group wins was at the prestigious Westminster Kennel Club Show in 1981, the first Briard to do this.

Though Ch. C'est Bonheur Woodbine Tinsel "only" won BIS once in 1988, her 19 Groups and 34 Group placements left her number 10 in the newly created Herding Group that year. She repeated that placement in 1989 with her impressive Group record, going first 14 times and placing on 29 occasions. Tinsel was three times Best of Breed at Westminster, placing in the Group once. In addition to these top wins, she was one of the foundations of the immensely successful Déjà Vu, where Tinsel grandchildren have

Ch. Déjà Vu In Like Flynn, the top-winning Briard in the U.S., shown winning BOB at Westminster in 2001, judged by Lester Mapes and handled by Davin McAteer.

won Best of Breed at Westminster continually from 1995 through 2001. The line breeds on successfully with a great-granddaughter winning in 2004.

Terry Miller, of Déjà Vu Briards, was training other breeds before she fell for the charm of the Briard, most especially the tawny ones. On her website (www.dejavubriards.com), she tells how she comes "into contact with huge numbers of dogs of all breeds, as well as many Briards. I can say unequivocally that Tinsel had the best temperament of any dog I have ever known. She was stable, friendly and constant. She was once described in the national dog press as the 'extroverted Briard bitch.' Even though she was sunny, with a wonderful enthusiasm for life, she was a Briard through and through. Her value to the breed was tremendous in her talent for reproducing her temperament, and

still in many generations removed we see her contribution.

"Lastly she was a gifted mover. Her structure and proportions permitted incredible suspended movement at the trot, with extreme reach and drive and the perfect movement coming and going, with beautiful alignment feet and hocks."

It is not surprising that with her outstanding hind movement she had puppies that scored well in the assessment of their hips for hip dysplasia by the Orthopedic Foundation for Animals (OFA). Tinsel was the product of two Phydeaux champions bred by Mary Lou Tingley, and her grandmother was the outstanding French import Ch. Jennie d'el Pastre.

The tawny bitch Ch. Déjà Vu House On Fire won Best of Breed at Westminster in 1996 and 1997, plus placed fourth in the Herding Group in 1997. Other Déjà Vu Best of Breed winners at Westminster include Ch. Déjà Vu Every Little Breeze in 1995, Ch. Déjà Vu In Like Flynn in 1998, 1999, 2000 (Group 3) and 2001, Ch.

Déjà Vu Nine to Five in 2002 and the In Like Flynn daughter Ch. Déjà Vu Ruffles Have Ridges in 2004.

In Like Flynn holds the record for more wins in the show rings of the US than any other Briard. He was BIS all-breeds 15 times, winner of the Herding Group 105 times and placed in the group on 270 occasions.

Unfortunately the Phillips System stopped in 1990, having generated many other systems for calculating the top-winning show dogs, all of them slightly different. None of these systems have the "gravitas" of the original one, often each producing different top dogs in each breed. Very few dogs win top all-systems, but Flynn is one, achieving top Briard all-systems in 1998 and 1999, fourth Herding Dog in 1998, fifth Herding Dog in 1999 and winning one point system for Briards in 2000.

Ch. Déjà Vu Purple People Eater, shown winning BIS at Rockland County KC in 2005 under judge Ralph Ambrosio, handled by Regina Keiter.

Briards are successful in the show ring, but they haven't lost their love for herding and guarding work.

A RUGGED SHEPHERD DOG

In *A History of Herding Briards in the USA*, Mary Weir-Anderson of Enchanted Briards refers to the Briard as being, first and foremost, a rugged shepherd dog. It is in his blood and it is not unusual to observe this herding ability in Briards who have never seen a sheep. The following paragraph is Noel Wanlen's thesis on the Briard, written in 1946:

"Perhaps you know a Briard who adores to sit on your feet, the trait so important to Jehan de Brie in 1541; or one who lowers his head and 'gives you the eye;' or who knows the exact boundaries of his property, whether marked or not; who will nudge with his head to gain attention and if ignored, will bump harder; who will press with his shoulder to direct a child away from the street; who never leaves your sight when you go for a walk, running back frequently to your side; who will circle a group of children in the yard, going to the side away from the house to watch; or one who runs in 'squares,' gleefully squaring his corners; or one who never considers using his teeth, except to gently pinch with his front teeth to show affection; or a special dog who places himself between a child and the parent who is losing patience; who will not settle down for the night until everyone is safely in bed, then sleeps across the doorway to guard against intruders; and chooses as his favorite spot, a place where he can watch most of the household activities, quietly following behind when you go to another part of the house."

Many behavioral traits that owners observe in their Briards parallel so closely the work of the flock dog that their inheritance cannot be denied. They persist even in Briards who are several generations down from their sheep-herding ancestors. The herding traits that are so valued inspired Briarders throughout the years to promote herding programs.

BRIARD HERDING HISTORY

Herding ability comes naturally to both veteran and puppy Briards.

According to breeder Mary Weir-Anderson's piece that appeared in the March/April 1998 issue of *The Herdsman,* Briards were used in all types of herding situations as farm dogs. They were responsible for keeping the sheep moving along the grass strips between the crops, protecting these crops and then returning the sheep at night to the farm. Then at the farm, the Briard helped the farmer with the chores.

In some areas of France that had wide grazing pastures, the Briard worked beside one or two other breeds to keep the large flocks from straying. At night, the Briard was a vigilant watchdog protecting the sheep and the shepherds. Rumor has it Briards were brought to the United States by Thomas Jefferson and the Marquis de Lafayette to herd their sheep.

BRIARD

IS THE BRIARD FOR YOU?

It is a big step to decide on a Briard as a pet, as he is large and, if not kept under control, can be exceptionally boisterous. Indeed, the main reason that Briards are given up to breed rescue services by their owners is that they are out of control. This is not in an aggressive way, but in an over-enthusiastic, bouncing and destroying-the-house sort of a way. They are too large to let run wild.

A Briard also needs some work on his coat if it is to remain beautiful. Also keep in mind that a Briard is a large dog to handle in the bath and can make the house very wet when he jumps out of the tub to avoid the towels.

Because their initial function was the guarding and droving of sheep, Briards make very good guardians of the family and home. They get along very well with the family children but are less sociable with strangers. Briards can try to dominate other dogs they meet and at times may even challenge familiar people to see if they can become the pack leaders of their homes.

A dog like a Greyhound is very lazy inside the house but a whirlwind of activity out of doors. Not so with the Briard— he is a whirlwind everywhere, and his big mud-encrusted feet have caused the demise of many a light-colored fabric.

Training is absolutely vital for the Briard, and training experts consider the breed to be a little slow on the uptake when compared to German Shepherd Dogs or Border Collies. Maybe this is because the Briard had to do *some* thinking while protecting its livestock, but not as much problem-solving as the Border Collie, who performs

ORIGINAL PURPOSE

To understand any breed of dog, you have to think about the job for which it was bred. Briards and the other French sheepdogs were developed for a type of sheep farming called transhumance. This means moving the sheep long distances from winter to summer pastures, and the moving flocks may have consisted of thousands of sheep. Work like this requires a dog with a bit of independent thinking.

HYPOTHYROIDISM
The Briard is among the many breeds in which hypothyroidism is seen. Breeders are urged to test all breeding stock to minimize its occurence.

quite complex tasks in moving his sheep. Regardless, training the Briard has to start early and continue at a steady pace.

HEALTH CONSIDERATIONS

One of the benefits of breeding in small numbers is that health considerations have a higher profile. The number of health problems that are documented for the Briard will depend on what source you consult. Some lists include every illness that has ever been seen in the breed and do not really give an idea of how common each one is. The health problems discussed later in this book are bloat, or gastric torsion, found in all breeds with large, deep chests (discussed in the feeding section); hip dysplasia, also found in nearly all large breeds; and retinal pigment epithelial dystrophy and stationary night blindness, which are eye diseases (the latter three conditions are discussed in the healthcare chapter).

When obtaining a puppy, make sure that your pet's parents are clear of any eye disease and that the x-rays of their hips were

as good or better than the average for Briards. Bloat is a dreadful condition and much research is taking place on this problem that can kill an otherwise healthy dog in a matter of hours.

COLORS

Briard colors typically are black, gray and tawny. A range of shades is seen, as the AKC permits all uniform colors other than white. However, the situation is actually much more complicated than this, and the only way to simplify the matter of color is to look at Briard color genetics. Honestly, it is genetics that makes the true color situation easier to understand. I do realize that the most difficult part of discussing the topic of Briard color genetics is to convince the reader not to skip over this part of the chapter! Although the word "genetics" has an aura about it that says "this bit is only for brain surgeons and nuclear physicists," that is just not the case.

The key to Briard color genetics is that two dogs that are the same color may have ended up this way despite having different genes. Any Briard inherits half of his genetic make-up from his sire and half from his dam. The genetic material is inherited as little lumps of chemicals called genes.

I find that the best analogy for genes is to consider each gene as a book that can be borrowed from the library. Each gene is a book, a separate entity, but it also belongs to a group of books on a similar subject. Each pile of books, such as the pile of cook books or the pile of westerns, is the equivalent of what is called a gene series. The gene series can contain many different genes; a series can be large, like the huge pile of cook books, or it may be very small, like the number of books written on photographing goldfish.

The rules of this library are that the borrower has to take one book from each pile as a present from mother and another from each pile as a present from father, in the same way that a gene from each series is inherited by the Briard from sire and dam.

HEART-HEALTHY

In this modern age of ever-improving cardio-care, no doctor or scientist can dispute the advantages of owning a dog to lower a person's risk of heart disease. Studies have proven that petting a dog, walking a dog and grooming a dog all show positive results toward lowering your blood pressure. The simple routine of exercising your dog—going outside with the dog and walking, jogging or playing catch—is heart-healthy in and of itself. If you are normally less active than your physician thinks you should be, adopting a dog may be a smart option to improve your own quality of life as well as that of another creature.

To make things more interesting, the borrower can take a copy of the same book from father and from mother. For

Illustrated Briard with at least one gene that is B.

Illustrated Briard that would have to be bb.

the Briard, this would be inheriting the same gene from both his sire and dam. In this case, the dog is said to be homozygous for this gene (homo, meaning "same" and zygous, meaning "new individual").

The borrower could take two different books from the pile. In this case, for the Briard, he would be inheriting two different genes from the same series, one from each parent. For this gene, the dog would be called heterozygous, from hetero, meaning "different."

THE B OR BLACK SERIES
The first category is the B or black series. The gene b is rarely present in the Briard: most are BB. The gene B must be present for black pigment to be made. When B is present, we see the color black in the Briard. This gene is expressed as black nose,

> **INTUITIVE BEHAVIOR**
> Though the Briard can be boisterous, if there are old, infirm or very young children about they behave in a much more gentle way. Briards have been kind and affectionate visitors to old people's homes, and they have been seen to communicate with autistic children in a way that no human could.

black lips, black eyelids and any black in the coat. The gene B covers the presence of the gene b. In genetic terms, B is dominant to b; b is recessive to B.

A Briard that happens to be Bb would be indistinguishable from the BB dog in appearance because B is the dominant gene. The Bb dog would still have a black nose, black lips and black eyelids. However, a Briard that was bb would be incapable of making the color black.

Illustrated Briard with at least one gene that is D.

Illustrated Briard that would have to be dd.

SOME PET FACTS

- 94% of pet owners keep a pet's photo on display in their home or office.
- 46% of pets sleep on their owners' beds.
- 63% of pet owners celebrate our pets' birthdays.
- 66% of pet owners take our pets to the vet more often than we see our own physicians!

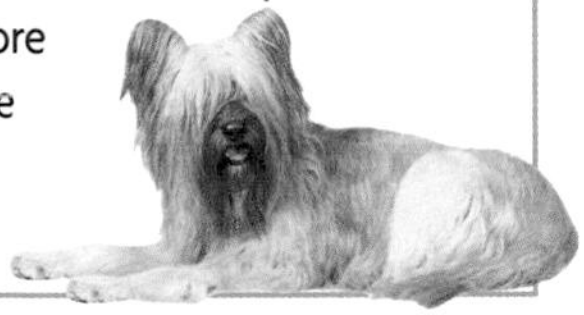

Anywhere that should have been black would be liver or chocolate, so it would have a liver nose, lips and eyelids.

Liver-colored Pointers and chocolate Labradors have this bb conformation. Liver-colored dogs cannot have black noses.

The D or Dilution Series

The next category is the D or dilution series. There are just two genes in this series: D, which is dominant to d, and d, which is recessive to D. If a Briard has the gene D, the pigment will be seen at its full intensity; in other words, black will be black. The Dd dog will be indistinguishable in appearance from the DD dog because the D is dominant.

A Briard that is dd has the pigment in each hair reduced. There is not full color, but dilute color. Black appears as blue, and liver appears as yellow. As liver is not found in the Briard, its dilute form is not found either.

The blue dog cannot have a black nose, so his nose, lips and eyelids are blue.

There are two types of black Briard, the homozygous form (DD) and the heterozygous form (Dd). There is only one form of blue dog, dd. When geneticists try to predict what might result from a mating, they write out the genes available in a square. If a DD dog was mated to a dd dog, we would have:

Homozygous blue (dd)

		d	d
Homozygous black (DD)	D	Dd	Dd
	D	Dd	Dd

This mating gives only one color, heterozygous black. All these puppies appear black just like their black parent, but if two of them were mated together we would have a 25% chance of breeding a blue, as shown in the following square:

Heterozygous black (Dd)

		D	d
Heterozygous black (Dd)	D	DD	Dd
	d	Dd	dd

A: Dominant black, the puppy is born black and stays black.

a^y: Dominant yellow, the puppy is born sable, but this fades to leave yellow on the adult dog.

This brings us to the problem of population genetics. The very first genetic experiments were done by an Austrian monk named Gregor Mendel, who used pea plants. He carried out thousands of pea matings before publishing his original paper in 1865, which was shamefully disregarded during his lifetime. It was only because he had worked with so many pea plants that his calculations worked out exactly. Since Briard litters thankfully do not contain hundreds of puppies, we do not get perfect ratios. We cannot predict the number of puppies of each color born, but we can predict which colors are possible.

Therefore, when two heterozygous blacks are mated together, all that we can say for certain is that the mating could produce homozygous black, heterozygous black and homozygous blue puppies. The two types of black appear exactly the same in color, and probably there will not be many blues.

THE A OR AGOUTI SERIES

This gene series is named after a South American rodent called an agouti, which looks a little like a giant guinea pig. Agoutis are a sable-type color, and this series of genes includes the color sable.

The standard textbook description of this gene series

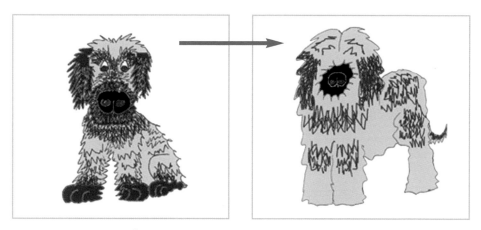

a^g: The puppy is born sable and remains sable as an adult.

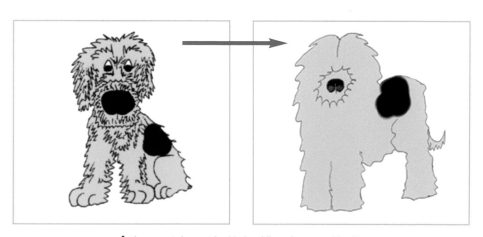

a^s: The puppy is born with a black saddle and grows up like this.

a^t: The puppy is born black and tan (like a Beauceron) and remains like this.

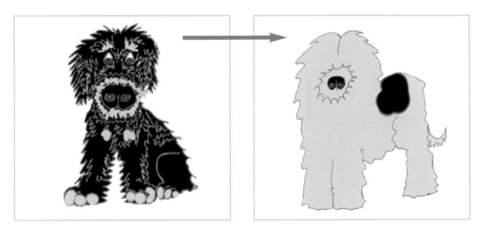

a^a: The puppy is born black and tan but develops a saddle as an adult dog (like an Airedale Terrier).

gives five genes, but it is possible that it is more complex than this, especially in the case of the Briard. The usual five are:

A: dominant black—the puppy is born black and stays completely black;

a^y: dominant yellow—the puppy is born sable but at adulthood the black has faded, leaving the coat completely yellow;

a^g: the puppy is born sable and remains sable;

a^s: the puppy is born with a saddle of black with extensive yellow and remains like this;

a^t: the puppy is born black

and tan like a Beauceron and remains like this.

There must be at least one other gene in this series, one which the Airedale Terrier has, which causes the puppy to be born with the coloration like that of a Beauceron, but the color changes to just a saddle of dark color. Perhaps we should name this gene a^a: the puppy is born the black and tan of a Beauceron and fades in color to the black and tan of an adult Airedale Terrier. To work out where this comes in as far as being dominant/recessive, we would need data from matings of dogs of this color.

However, we do not want all of these genes in the Briard. We have A, a^y, a^g and a tiny remnant population of a^t that everyone has been trying to eradicate for over 100 years. It does not seem that a^s and a^a are

The black and tan of the Airedale puppy shown here differs from the black and tan coloration of the Beauceron.

E: Not having a mask

E ^{m} : Having a black mask.

present in the breed.

With so many genes for sable available and the possibility of their "mixing and matching" together (heterozygous arrangements), no wonder there are so many different shades of fawn in the Briard.

THE E OR EXTENSION OF BLACK INTO THE COAT SERIES

There are two genes in this series that affect the Briard:

E^m: having a black mask (and ears);

E: not having a black mask.

Most fawn Briards have the black points. It is not possible to see if a black Briard has a black mask.

THE G OR GRAYING SERIES

Just as with all of the subtle sable fawns, there is a gene series that affects the intensity of the color of black. The gene G causes graying of the coat—not the gradual graying of age, but the graying that is found in breeds like the Bedlington Terrier, in which the coat progressively changes in color until it has become a blue shade. However, the nose, eyelids and lips remain black.

The two genes in this series are G, giving graying, which is dominant to g, in which the color remains the same and does not go gray.

The two genes give three combinations:

GG: born black, coat fades to gray/blue, nose remains black;

GG: Born black, coat fades to blue, nose stays black.

Gg: born black, coat fades to gray/blue, nose remains black;
gg: born black, stays black.

THE BLUE PROBLEM

We have demonstrated the different ways that a Briard can be blue, either by the dilution gene d or by the graying gene G. Some describe the d blue as "blue born blue" and the G blue as "blue born black." The problem with the d blue is that it cannot have a black nose, which is against the edicts of the standard. Perhaps it is time for the senior breeders of the world to consider the genetic impossibility of a dog of a recognized color having a black nose.

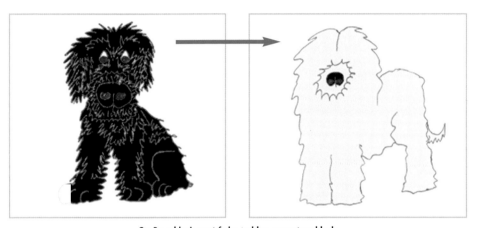

Gg: Born black, coat fades to blue, nose stays black.

gg: Born black, and remains black as an adult.

As for the G for graying with the fawns, this just adds to the possibilities of a myriad of shades.

The American Kennel Club's breed standard states that all uniform colors (other than white) are permissible and deeper shades of each are preferred, listing the colors as black, shades of gray and shades of tawny. Combinations of color are allowed as long as the transition from one to the next is gradual. As we can see, the situation is a little more complex than these few lines indicate.

BRIARD PERSONALITY
In regard to personality, Mary Weir-Anderson of Enchanted

Fawn is the most commonly seen color in the Briard, though blacks are also seen, as well as the rarer gray coloration.

Briards writes, "Briards seem to exhibit two basic types of herding personality: the very biddable, sometimes 'woozy' Briard and the hard-headed 'show me' alpha Briard. These types are not necessarily sex divisions. Type #1 can be herded easily if trained slowly, and the handler must be cautious, constantly boosting the confidence level. These Briards usually work at greater distances, may bark and are not comfortable in close contact with the stock. For these reasons a lot of pen close-contact work and cheerleading-type herding is needed to increase their confidence and usage of their power.

"Type #2 Briards need a talented, fair, alpha leader. These Briards must be taught the rules of the game and the consequences of breaking those rules. The handler must be firm and in total control until eventually a partnership evolves. This type should never be herded seriously at a young age.

"The Briard learns best when he is of an age to take correction positively. When started too young the Briard can learn bad habits that are hard to erase and can't be corrected with punishment, as the dog is too immature to understand. Circling, chasing and impatience are a few of these bad habits."

The blue Briard has a blue nose due to his being homozygous for the dilution gene d.

BRIARD

Breed standards were devised in Britain during the Victorian era, after the development of the dog show. Dog shows spread to France in 1863, just four years after the first recorded show was held in Newcastle, Britain. The first Briard standard was drawn up by the members of the Club Français du Chien du

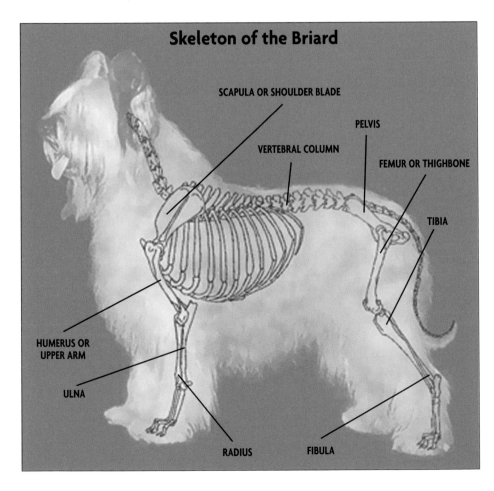

Skeleton of the Briard

- SCAPULA OR SHOULDER BLADE
- PELVIS
- VERTEBRAL COLUMN
- FEMUR OR THIGHBONE
- TIBIA
- HUMERUS OR UPPER ARM
- ULNA
- RADIUS
- FIBULA

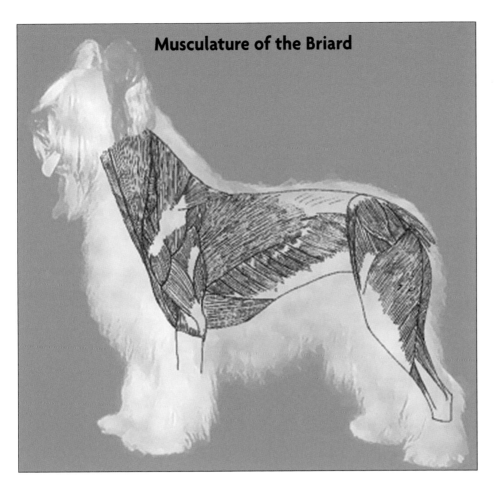

Musculature of the Briard

Berger (French Club for Sheepdogs) in 1897. The president of this club was Monsieur Boulet, a gentleman who was interested in gundogs as well as sheepdogs and who created the breed named after him, the Boulet Griffon, which can be considered as a sort of French wire-haired pointer.

The breeding and showing of pedigreed dogs was an activity mainly carried out by those with a sufficient amount of money to have a substantial amount of leisure time. At that time, people also had a better knowledge of animal construction than we have today because the principal modes of transport during their lifetimes had involved horses. If the horse was not correctly constructed, then the chances were that the people would not get to where they were going.

Any description that uses just words is open to many interpretations, and we have to work harder to envision what the breed standard means because we start with a lot less "instinctive" knowledge than those who first wrote the standard.

The most outstanding dogs will win under all judges; opinions tend to differ when it comes to the faulty dogs. The all-rounder judge will tend to give first place to the dog with the best conformation, while the breed specialist will have problems giving a prize to this dog if his tail did not have the characteristic hooked tip or if there is something wrong with the double dewclaws, two of the special features of the breed.

AMERICAN KENNEL CLUB BREED STANDARD FOR THE BRIARD

General Appearance
A dog of handsome form. Vigorous and alert, powerful without coarseness, strong in bone and muscle, exhibiting the strength and agility required of the herding dog. Dogs lacking these qualities, however concealed by the coat, are to be penalized.

Size, Proportions
Size—males 23 to 27 inches at the withers; bitches 22 to 25.5 inches at the withers. *Disqualification*—all dogs or bitches under the minimum. *Proportions*—the Briard is not cobby in build. In males the length of the body, measured from the point of the shoulder to the point of the buttock, is equal to or slightly more than his height at the withers. The female may be a little longer.

BETTER THAN THE AVERAGE DOG
Even though you may never show your dog, you should still read the breed standard. The breed standard tells you more than just physical specifications such as how tall your dog should be; it also describes how he should act, how he should move and what unique qualities make him the breed that he is. You are not investing money in a pure-bred dog so that you can own a dog that "sort of looks like" the breed you're purchasing. You want a typical, handsome representative of the breed, one that all of your friends and family and people you meet out in public will recognize as the breed you've so carefully selected and researched. If the parents of your prospective puppy bear little or no resemblance to the dog described in the breed standard, you should keep searching!

Head

The head of a Briard always gives the impression of length, having sufficient width without being cumbersome. The correct length of a good head, measured from the occiput to the tip of the nose, is about 40% of the height of the dog at the withers. There is no objection to a slightly longer head, especially if the animal tends to a longer body line. Viewed from above, from the front or in profile, the fully-coated silhouette gives the impression of two rectangular forms, equal in length but differing in height and width, blending together rather abruptly. The larger rectangle is the skull and the other forms the muzzle. The head joins the neck in a right angle and is held proudly alert. The head is sculptured in clean lines, without jowls or excess flesh on the sides, or under the eyes or temples. *Expression*—the gaze is frank, questioning and confident. *Eyes*—the eyes set well apart with the inner corners and outer corners on the same level. Large, well opened and calm, they must never be narrow or slanted. The color must be black or black-brown with very dark pigmentation of the rim of the eyelids, whatever the color of the coat. *Disqualification*—yellow eyes or spotted eyes. *Ears*—the ears

Briards entered in dog shows are compared to the breed standard. The Briard that most closely conforms to the standard, in the judge's opinion, is selected as Best of Breed.

should be attached high, have thick leather and be firm at the base. Low-set ears cause the head to appear to be too arched. The length of the natural ear should be equal to or slightly less than one-half the length of the head, always straight and covered with long hair. The natural ear must not lie flat against the head and, when alert, the ears are lifted slightly, giving a square look to the top of the skull. The ears when cropped should be carried

This Beauceron shows head proportions that would be correct for a Briard.

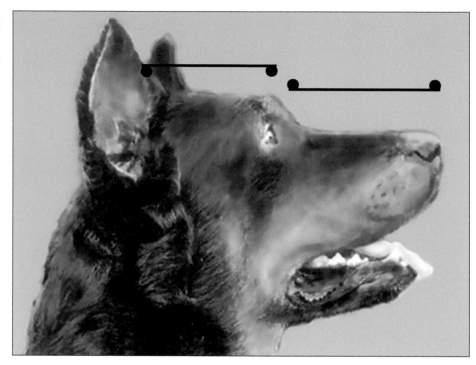

This Beauceron has a skull that is far too curved; the two lines making the top of the skull are far from parallel.

upright and parallel, emphasizing the parallel lines of the head; when alert, they should face forward, well open with long hair falling over the opening. The cropped ear should be long, broad at the base, tapering gradually to a rounded tip. *Skull*—the width of the head, as measured across the skull, is slightly less than the length of the skull from the occiput to the stop. Although not clearly visible on the fully-coated head, the occiput is prominent and the forehead is very slightly rounded. *Muzzle*—the muzzle with mustache and beard is somewhat wide and terminates in a right angle. The muzzle must not be narrow or

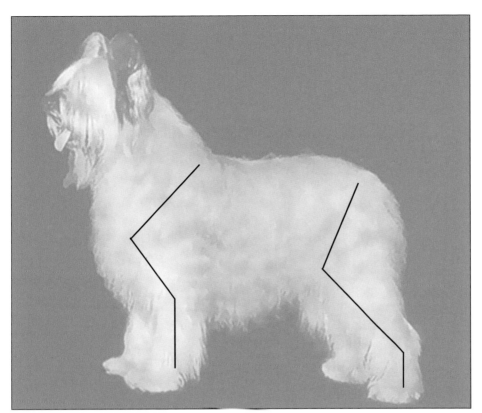

Correct angulation in the Briard.

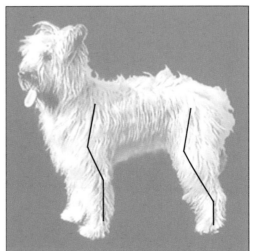

The dog on the left has poor hind angulation. He would walk the same way you would if you did not bend your knees, and there is no way he could perform his daily duties as a herder with this construction. The dog on the right has equally poor angulation in both the fore- and hind-quarters.

The Briard's gait should be effortless and strong with plenty of drive. Exhibitors must move their dogs in the show ring to demonstrate that the dogs possess the desired gait.

pointed. *Planes*—the topline of the muzzle is parallel to the topline of the skull, and the junction of the two forms a well-marked stop, which is midway between the occiput and the tip of the nose, and on a level with the eyes. *Nose*—square rather than round, always black with nostrils well opened. *Disqualification*—any color other than black. *Lips*—the lips are of medium thickness, firm of line and fitted neatly, without folds or flews at the corners. The lips are black. *Bite, Teeth*—strong, white and adapting perfectly in a scissors bite.

Neck, Topline and Body
Neck—strong and well constructed. The neck is in the shape of a truncated cone, clearing the shoulders well. It is strongly muscled and has good length. *Topline*—the Briard is constructed with a very slight incline, downward from the prominent withers to the back which is straight, to the broad loin and the croup which is slightly inclined. The croup is well muscled and slightly sloped to give a well-rounded finish. The topline is strong, never swayed nor roached. *Body*—the chest is broad and deep with moderately curved

ribs, egg-shaped in form, the ribs not too rounded. The breastbone is moderately advanced in front, descending smoothly to the level of the elbows and shaped to give good depth to the chest. The abdomen is moderately drawn up but still presents good volume. *Tail*—uncut, well feathered, forming a crook at the extremity, carried low and not deviating to the right or to the left. In repose, the bone of the tail descends to the point of the hock, terminating in the crook, similar in shape to the printed "J" when viewed from the dog's right side. In action, the tail is raised in a harmonious curve, never going above the level of the back, except for the terminal crook. *Disqualification*—tail non-existent or cut.

Four Briards, two with cropped ears and two with natural drop ears. All are good, sound examples of the breed. Note the good hooked tail on the cropped black dog. The balance of the uncropped fawn dog has been a little lost because the dog is slightly too outstretched.

Forequarters

Shoulder blades are long and sloping forming a 45-degree angle with the horizontal, firmly attached by strong muscles and blending smoothly with the withers. *Legs*—the legs are powerfully muscled with strong bone. The forelegs are vertical when viewed from the side except the pasterns are very slightly inclined. Viewed from the front or rear, the legs are straight and parallel to the median line of the body, never turned inward or outward. The distance between the front legs is equal to the distance between the rear legs. The construction of the legs is of utmost importance, determining the dog's ability to work and his

> ### SNIPEY
> A snipe is a game bird that would have often been seen on the dinner tables of 19th-century aristocracy. It has a long pointed nose; thus the term "snipiness" refers to a muzzle with a lack of strength in the underjaw. The Briard has a strong jaw to go with its big strong white teeth.

resistance to fatigue. *Dewclaws*—dewclaws on the forelegs may or may not be removed. *Feet*—strong and rounded, being slightly oval in shape. The feet travel straight forward in the line of movement. The toes are strong, well arched and compact. The pads are well developed, compact and elastic, covered with strong tissue. The nails are always black and hard.

Hindquarters

The hindquarters are powerful, providing flexible, almost tireless movement. The pelvis slopes at a 30-degree angle from the horizontal and forms a right angle with the upper leg bone. *Legs* viewed from the side, the legs are well angulated with the metatarsus slightly inclined, the hock making an angle of 135 degrees. *Dewclaws*—two dewclaws are required on each rear leg, placed low on the leg, giving a wide base to the foot.

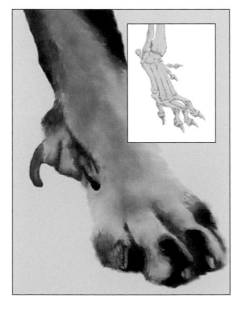

The double dewclaw on the back legs of a Beauceron. The Briard has this same structure. The inset shows the skeletal appearance of the double dewclaw. The two dewclaws are made of three bones each, with the nail at the end.

Occasionally the nail may break off completely. The dog shall not be penalized for the missing nail so long as the digit itself is present. Ideally the dewclaws form additional functioning toes. *Disqualification*—anything less than two dewclaws on each rear leg. *Feet*—if the rear toes turn out very slightly when the hocks and metatarsus are parallel, then the position of the feet is correct.

Correct topline on the Briard. A firm, level back has the strongest muscles to help the Briard work all day.

Coat

The outer coat is coarse, hard and dry (making a dry rasping sound between the fingers). It lies down flat, falling naturally in long, slightly waving locks, having the sheen of good health. On the shoulders the length of the hair is generally six inches or more. The undercoat is fine and tight on all the body. The head is well covered with hair which lies down, forming a natural part in the center. The eyebrows do not lie flat but, instead, arch up and out in a curve that lightly veils the eyes. The hair is never so abundant that it masks the form of the head or completely covers the eyes.

Roached topline (computer-generated fault).

Color

All uniform colors are permitted except white. The colors are black, various shades of gray and various shades of tawny.

Dippy topline (computer-generated fault).

This tail is incorrect for a Briard as it has no hook on the end.

This tail is of proper shape and is carried correctly in repose, resembling a "J."

The deeper shades of each color are preferred. Combinations of two of these colors are permitted, provided there are no marked spots and the transition from one color to another takes place gradually and symmetrically. The only permissible white: white hairs scattered throughout the coat and/or a white spot on the chest not to exceed one inch in diameter at the root of the hair. *Disqualification*—white coat, spotted coat, white spot on chest exceeding one inch in diameter.

Gait
The well-constructed Briard is a marvel of supple power. His movement has been described as "quicksilver," permitting him to make abrupt turns, springing starts and sudden stops required of the sheepherding dog. His gait is supple and light, almost like that of a large feline. The gait gives the impression that the dog glides along without touching the ground. Strong, flexible movement is essential to the sheepdog. He is above all a trotter, single-tracking, occasionally galloping and he frequently needs to change his speed to accomplish his work. His conformation is harmoniously balanced and strong to sustain him in the long day's work. Dogs with clumsy or inelegant gait must be penalized.

Temperament
He is a dog of heart, with spirit and initiative, wise and fearless with no trace of timidity. Intelligent, easily trained, faithful, gentle and obedient, the Briard possesses an excellent memory and an ardent desire to please his master. He retains a high degree of his ancestral instinct to guard home and master. Although he is reserved with strangers, he is loving and loyal to those he knows. Some will display a certain independence.

Disqualifications
- All dogs or bitches under the minimum size limits.
- Yellow eyes or spotted eyes.
- Nose any color other than black.
- Tail non-existent or cut.
- Less than two dewclaws on each rear leg.
- White coat.
- Spotted coat.
- White spot on chest exceeding one inch in diameter.

Approved February 8, 1975
Reformatted January 12, 1992

COMMENTS ON THE STANDARD
As with any breed standard, it would not be possible to read it to a particularly artistic person with no knowledge of dogs and have them draw a Briard. It is

DEWCLAWS IN FRANCE

In France, there are very strict rules about the structure of the dewclaws, as not every Briard has them as fully formed as in the ideal structure illustrated here. It is permissible to have the bones of the two toes fused together, and it is permissible to have the two proximal phalanges missing (giving "floating dewclaws"). If two phalanges are missing from one dewclaw, it is not permissible for the dog to be awarded the CAC, the certificate necessary for the title of French Champion. If four phalanges are missing, the dog would be disqualified in France.

doubtful that he would be able to manage drawing something even resembling a dog. This is because those who drew up the standard were so immersed in livestock that they had a large amount of implicit knowledge, information that was so much a part of them that they did not realize that future generations would not instinctively know what they meant.

The whole object of a breed standard is to describe a dog that has both perfect conformation and breed points. What is perfect conformation? It means that all of the bones are correctly formed and join together at the joints at the correct angles so they can flex and move in the most efficient way. This results in a dog that seems to move with no effort, a dog that could run after sheep from dawn to dusk.

What are breed points? These are the features that say "I am a Briard." All dogs should have perfect conformation, but only a Briard has the combination of the hook at the end of its tail, the double dewclaws and a head formed from rectangles that are covered with Briard-quality hair in a Briard way.

It is not as easy to see the structure of the head of the Briard as it is to see the structure of the head of a breed such as a Borzoi because of the Briard's profuse coat. The way to find out what really is going on under all that hair is to gently feel the proportions. The stop (the indentation at the eyes) should be halfway from the back of the skull (the occiput) to the nose. The standard describes very well the rectangles that form the head, and if we look at pictures of what is effectively the smooth-haired Briard, the Beauceron, we can see them. The heads of both the Briard and the Beauceron demonstrate horizontally placed eyes and a large

Eye color affects the expression. The dark eye, as required by the standard, gives a much kinder expression. The Briard's eye on the right has been altered by computer to appear light.

The head of the Beauceron demonstrates the horizontally placed eyes, as in the Briard as well, and the large nose. From the front, the muzzle forms a smaller rectangle within the large square of the head.

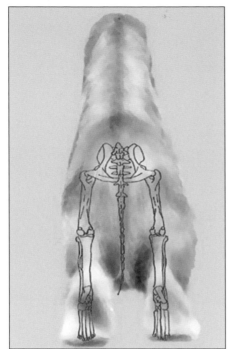

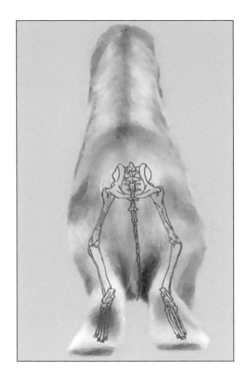

Rear view of the Briard (computer-generated illustration). The dog on the upper left has correct hindlegs; the whole assembly is more or less parallel. The dog on the upper right demonstrates cowhocks, where the bones forming the hocks veer towards each other. The dog below has bow hocks, the joints being widely separated from each other.

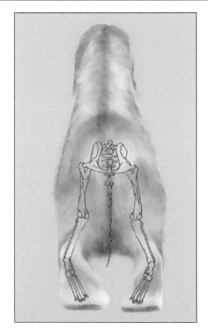

nose. From the front, the muzzle forms a smaller rectangle within the larger square of the whole head.

Eye color affects the Briard's expression. The dark eye, as required by the standard, gives a much kinder expression than a light eye. The Briard should possess a correct scissors bite, in which the upper teeth closely overlap the lower ones, giving an efficient cutting bite.

Cropped ears are "upright and parallel," while uncropped ears lie at the sides of the head. They are very mobile ears, expressing the dog's emotions.

Wide front.

Narrow front.

Correct front.

The uncropped ears of the Briard lie close to the sides of the head.

BRIARD

If you are absolutely sure that the Briard is the breed for you, then it is important to realize the amount of work that goes into making a member of this breed physically and mentally presentable to the rest of the world. As with all larger breeds, the growth curve is from puppy until the age of 18 months (adult), from adult until the age of 7 or 8 years and from then on, a senior dog. Every day after the age of 11 is an extra blessing.

It is possible to obedience-train your Briard to a high standard, but it will be harder than going through the same training program with a breed like the Border Collie. A Briard gets bored if asked to perform the same task repeatedly and will often refuse after doing something three or four times.

All dogs like consistency, so you must use the same commands for the same requested behavior. For example, the word "down" should have a specific meaning to your puppy and should be used in the same way by all household members. In other words, "down" should not mean "lie on the ground" when you say it, "stop jumping up" when the children say it and "get off the sofa" when granny says it. If one word is used for all of these things, not only will your puppy not understand but he also will be utterly confused. Your Briard will want to please you, so you will need to demonstrate clearly and consistently to your puppy what behavior is acceptable.

In the beginning, there will be a period of settling in, and you must be prepared for some mishaps around the home during the first few weeks of your life together. It will be important that your precious ornaments are kept well out of harm's (meaning the puppy's) way, and you will have

Of course you'll want to take the whole litter home, but work closely with the breeder to determine which Briard puppy will be the best fit for your household.

FIRST CAR RIDE

The ride to your home from the breeder will most likely be your puppy's first automobile experience, and you should make every effort to keep him comfortable and secure. Bring a large towel or small blanket for the puppy to lie on during the trip and an extra towel in case the pup gets carsick or has a potty accident. It's best to have another person with you to hold the puppy in his lap. Most puppies will fall fast asleep from the rolling motion of the car. If the ride is lengthy, you may have to stop so that the puppy can relieve himself, so be sure to bring a leash and collar for those stops. Avoid rest areas for potty trips, since those are frequented by many dogs, who may carry parasites or disease. It's better to stop at grassy areas near gas stations or shopping centers to prevent unhealthy exposure for your pup.

to think twice about where you place hot cups of coffee or anything breakable. Accidents can and do happen, so you will need to think ahead so as to avoid them. Electric cords must be carefully concealed, and your puppy must be taught where he can and cannot go.

Before making your commitment to a new puppy, think carefully about your future vacation plans. Your dog may or may not be able to travel abroad with you. If you have thought things through carefully and discussed the matter thoroughly with all members of your family, hopefully you will come to the right decision. If you decide that a Briard should join your family, this will hopefully be a happy, long-term relationship for all parties concerned.

BUYING A BRIARD PUPPY

Although you may be looking for a Briard as a pet dog rather than as a show dog, this does not mean that you want a dog that is in any way "second-rate." A caring breeder will have brought up the entire litter of puppies with the same amount of dedication, and a

A responsible breeder will first gauge if the Briard is the right breed for you and then what member of her litter is best suited for your home.

puppy destined for a pet home should be just as healthy as one that hopes to end up in the show ring.

Because you have carefully selected this breed, you will want a Briard that is a typical specimen, in both looks and temperament. In your endeavors to find such a puppy, you will have to select the breeder with care. The Briard Club of America can refer you to member breeders across the country and let you know about litters that are possibly available. However, although they can point you in the right direction, it will be up to you to do your homework carefully.

Even though you are probably not looking for a show dog, it is always a good idea to visit a large show so that you may see quality specimens of the breed. This will also give you an opportunity to meet breeders who should be able to answer some of your queries. In addition, you will get some idea about which breeders appear to take most care of their stock and are likely to have given their puppies the best possible start in life. Something else you may be able to decide upon is which color appeals to you most, although this is purely personal preference.

When buying your puppy, you will need to know about vaccinations: which ones have been given already and which ones the puppy still needs. It is important that any injections already given by a veterinarian have been recorded and documented for proof. A worming routine is also vital for any young puppy, so the breeder should be able to tell you exactly what treatment has been given, when it was administered and how you should continue.

Clearly, when selecting a puppy, the one you choose must be in good condition. The coat should look healthy, and there should be no discharge from the eyes or nose. Ears should also be clean and, of course, there should be absolutely no signs of parasites. Check that the skin is healthy and free of rashes and any other irritations. Of course, the puppy you choose should not have any evidence of loose stool.

As in several other breeds, some Briard puppies have umbilical hernias, which can be seen as a small lump on the tummy where the umbilical cord

COST OF OWNERSHIP

The purchase price of your puppy is merely the first expense in the typical dog budget. Quality dog food, veterinary care (sickness and health maintenance), dog supplies and grooming costs will add up to big bucks every year. Can you adequately afford to support a canine addition to the family?

was attached. It is preferable not to have such a hernia on any puppy, and you should check for this at the outset. If a hernia is present, you should discuss its seriousness with the breeder. Most umbilical hernias are safe, but your vet should keep an eye on it in case an operation is needed.

Just a few words of warning: be very careful about where you purchase your puppy. Find your breeder through a reputable source, like a breed club, and visit the quarters in which the puppies are kept. Always insist that you

see the puppy's dam and, if possible, the sire. Frequently the sire will not be owned by the litter's breeder, but a photograph may be available for you to see. Ask if the breeder has any other of the puppy's relatives that you can meet. For example, there may be an older half-sister or half-brother on the premises, and it would be interesting for you to see how the relative has turned out: his eventual size, coat quality, temperament and so on.

Be sure, too, that if you decide to buy a puppy, all relevant documentation is provided at the time of sale. You will need a copy of the pedigree, preferably American Kennel Club registration documents, vaccination certificates and a feeding chart so that you know exactly how the puppy has been fed and how you should continue. The breeder also should show you health clearances on the pup's parents; tests for Briards include hip dysplasia, eye disease, hypothyroidism and a bleeding disorder called von Willebrand's disease.

A COMMITTED NEW OWNER

By now you should understand what makes the Briard a most unique and special dog, one that may fit nicely into your family and lifestyle. If you have researched breeders, you should be able to recognize a knowledgeable and responsible Briard breeder who cares not only about his pups but also about what kind of owner you will be. If you have

A well-bred and obedience-trained Briard can make a dependable home companion and guard.

SIGNS OF A HEALTHY PUPPY

Healthy puppies are robust little fellows who are alert and active, sporting shiny coats and supple skin. They should not appear lethargic, bloated or pot-bellied, nor should they have flaky skin or runny or crusted eyes or noses. Their stools should be firm and well formed, with no evidence of blood or mucus.

completed the final step in your new journey, you have found a litter, or possibly two, of quality Briard pups.

A visit with the puppies and their breeder should be an education in itself. Breed research, breeder selection and puppy visitation are very important aspects of finding the puppy of your dreams. Beyond that, these things also lay the foundation for a successful future with your pup. Puppy personalities within each litter vary, from

the shy and easygoing puppy to the one who is dominant and assertive, with most pups falling somewhere in between. By spending time with the puppies you will be able to recognize certain behaviors and what these behaviors indicate about each pup's temperament. Which type of pup will complement your family dynamics is best determined by observing the puppies in action within their "pack." Your breeder's expertise and recommendations are also valuable. Although you may fall in love with a bold and brassy male, the breeder may suggest that another pup would be best for you. The breeder's experience in rearing Briard pups and matching their temperaments with appropriate humans offers the best assurance that your pup will meet your needs and expectations. The type of puppy that you select is just as important as your decision that the Briard is the breed for you.

The decision to live with a Briard is a serious commitment and not one to be taken lightly. This puppy is a living sentient being that will be dependent on you for basic survival for his entire life. Beyond the basics of survival—food, water, shelter and protection—he needs much, much more. The new pup needs love, nurturing and a proper canine education to mold him into a

NEW RELEASES

Most breeders release their puppies between eight and ten weeks of age. A breeder who allows puppies to leave the litter at five or six weeks of age may be more concerned with profit than with the puppies' welfare. However, some breeders of show or working breeds may hold one or more top-quality puppies longer, occasionally until three or four months of age, in order to evaluate the puppies' career or show potential and decide which one(s) they will keep for themselves.

Puppies will start eating solid foods before leaving the breeder, and you will be responsible for continuing to provide your Briard with sound nutrition during his entire lifespan.

responsible, well-behaved canine citizen. Your Briard's health and good manners will need consistent monitoring and regular "tune-ups," so your job as a responsible dog owner will be ongoing throughout every stage of his life. If you are not prepared to accept these responsibilities and commit to them for the next decade, likely longer, then you are not prepared to own a dog of any breed.

Although the responsibilities of owning a dog may at times tax your patience, the joy of living with your Briard far outweighs the workload, and a well-mannered adult dog is worth your time and effort. Before your very eyes, your new charge will grow up to be your most loyal friend, devoted to you unconditionally.

YOUR BRIARD SHOPPING LIST

Just as expectant parents prepare a nursery for their baby, so should you ready your home for the arrival of your Briard pup. If you

have the necessary puppy supplies purchased and in place before he comes home, it will ease the puppy's transition from the warmth and familiarity of his mom and littermates to the brand-new environment of his new home and human family. You will be too busy to stock up and prepare your house after your pup comes home, that's for sure. Imagine how a pup must feel upon being transported to a strange new place. It's up to you to comfort him and to let your little pup know that he is going to be happy with you.

FOOD AND WATER BOWLS

Your puppy will need separate bowls for his food and water. Stainless steel pans are generally preferred over plastic bowls since they sterilize better and pups are less inclined to chew on the metal. Heavy-duty ceramic bowls are popular, but consider how often you will have to pick up those heavy bowls. Buy adult-sized pans, as your puppy will grow into them before you know it.

THE DOG CRATE

If you think that crates are tools of punishment and confinement for when a dog has misbehaved, think again. Most breeders and almost all trainers recommend a crate as the preferred house-training aid as well as for all-around puppy training and safety. Because dogs are natural den creatures that prefer cave-like environments, the benefits of crate use are many. The crate provides the puppy with his very own "safe house," a cozy place to sleep, take a break or seek comfort with a favorite toy; a travel aid to house your dog when on the road, at motels or at the vet's office; a training aid to help teach your puppy proper toileting habits; and a place of solitude when non-dog people happen to drop by and don't want a lively puppy—or even a well-behaved adult dog— saying hello or begging for attention.

Crates come in several types, although the wire crate and the fiberglass airline-type crate are the most popular. Both are safe and your puppy will adjust to either one, so the choice is up to you.

TEMPERAMENT ABOVE ALL ELSE

Regardless of breed, a puppy's disposition is perhaps his most important quality. It is, after all, what makes a puppy lovable and "livable." If the puppy's parents or grandparents are known to be snappy or aggressive, the puppy is likely to inherit those tendencies. That can lead to serious problems, such as the dog's becoming a biter, which can lead to eventual abandonment.

The wire crates offer better visibility for the pup as well as better ventilation. Many of the wire crates easily collapse into suitcase-size carriers. The fiberglass crates, similar to those used by the airlines for animal transport, are sturdier and more den-like. However, the fiberglass crates do not collapse and are less ventilated than a wire crate, which can be problematic in hot weather. Some of the newer crates

Pet shops offer a variety of crates that are suitable for your Briard. Pictured are the popular fabric mesh (left), wire (right) and fiberglass (top) varieties.

are made of heavy plastic mesh; they are very lightweight and fold up into slim-line suitcases. However, a mesh crate might not be suitable for a pup with manic chewing habits.

Don't bother with a puppy-sized crate. Although your Briard will be a wee fellow when you bring him home, he will grow up in the blink of an eye and your puppy crate will be useless. Purchase a crate that will accommodate an adult Briard. He will stand about 22–27 inches when full grown, so an extra-large crate will be necessary.

BEDDING AND CRATE PADS
Your puppy will enjoy some type of soft bedding in his "room" (the

crate), something he can snuggle into to feel cozy and secure. Old towels or blankets are good choices for a young pup, since he may (and probably will) have a toileting accident or two in the crate or decide to chew on the bedding material. Once he is fully trained and out of the early chewing stage, you can replace the puppy bedding with a permanent crate pad if you prefer. Crate pads and other dog beds run the gamut from inexpensive to high-end doggie-designer styles, but don't splurge on the good stuff until you are sure that your puppy is reliable and won't tear it up or make a mess on it.

PUPPY TOYS
Just as infants and older children require objects to stimulate their minds and bodies, puppies need toys to entertain their curious

brains, wiggly paws and achy teeth. A fun array of safe doggie toys will help satisfy your puppy's chewing instincts and distract him from gnawing on the leg of your antique chair or your new leather sofa. Most puppy toys are cute and look as if they would be a lot of fun, but not all are necessarily safe or good for your puppy, so use caution when you go puppy-toy shopping.

Briard puppies grow quickly and need the sturdiest toys as pups and adults. The best "chewcifiers" are nylon and hard rubber bones that are safe to gnaw on and come in sizes appropriate for all age groups and breeds. Be especially careful of natural bones, which can splinter or develop dangerous sharp edges; pups can easily swallow or choke on those bone splinters. Veterinarians often tell of surgical nightmares involving bits of splintered bone, because in addition to the danger of choking, the sharp pieces can damage the intestinal tract.

Similarly, rawhide chews, while a favorite of most dogs and puppies, can be equally dangerous. Pieces of rawhide are easily swallowed after they get soft and gummy from chewing, and dogs have been known to choke on pieces of ingested rawhide. Rawhide chews should be offered only when you can supervise the puppy.

TOYS 'R SAFE

The vast array of tantalizing puppy toys is staggering. Stroll through any pet shop or pet-supply outlet and you will see that the choices can be overwhelming. However, not all dog toys are safe or sensible. Most very young puppies enjoy soft woolly toys that they can snuggle with and carry around. (You know they have outgrown them when they shred them up!) Avoid toys that have buttons, tabs or other enhancements that can be chewed off and swallowed. Soft toys that squeak are fun, but make sure your puppy does not disembowel the toy and remove (and swallow) the squeaker. Toys that rattle or make noise can excite a puppy, but they present the same danger as the squeaky kind and so require supervision. Hard rubber toys that bounce can also entertain a pup, but make sure that the toy is too big for your pup to swallow.

Soft woolly toys are special puppy favorites. They come in a wide variety of cute shapes and sizes; some look like little stuffed animals. Puppies love to shake them up and toss them about or simply carry them around. Be careful of fuzzy toys that have button eyes or noses that your pup could chew off and swallow, and make sure that he does not disembowel a squeaky toy to remove the squeaker! Braided rope toys are similar in that they are fun to chew and toss around, but they shred easily and the strings are easy to swallow. The strings are not digestible and, if the puppy doesn't pass them in his stool, he could end up at the vet's office. As with rawhides, your puppy should be closely monitored with rope toys.

If you believe that your pup has ingested one of these unsafe objects, check his stools for the next couple of days to see if he passes them when he defecates. At the same time, also watch for signs of intestinal distress. A call to your veterinarian might be in order to get his advice and be on the safe side.

An all-time favorite toy for puppies (young and old!) is the empty gallon milk jug. Hard plastic juice containers—46 ounces or more—are also excellent. Such containers make lots of noise when they are batted about, and puppies go crazy with

delight as they play with them. However, they don't often last very long, so be sure to remove and replace them when they get chewed up on the ends.

A word of caution about homemade toys: be careful with your choices of non-traditional play objects. Never use old shoes or socks, since a puppy cannot distinguish between the old ones on which he's allowed to chew and the new ones in your closet that are strictly off limits. That principle applies to anything that resembles something that you don't want your puppy to chew.

COLLARS

Putting a collar on a puppy may be upsetting for him. Reassurance and gentle perseverance will soon make the pup comfortable with his collar on. A lightweight nylon collar is the best choice for a very young pup. Quick-click collars are easy to put on and remove, and they can be adjusted as the puppy grows. Introduce him to his collar as soon as he comes home to get him accustomed to wearing it. He'll get used to it quickly and won't mind a bit. Make sure that it is snug enough that it won't slip off, yet loose enough to be comfortable for the pup. You should be able to slip two fingers between the collar and his neck. Check the collar often, as puppies grow in spurts, and his collar can become too tight almost overnight.

Collaring Our Canines

The standard flat collar with a buckle or a snap, in leather, nylon or cotton, is widely regarded as the everyday all-purpose collar. If the collar fits correctly, you should be able to fit two fingers between the collar and the dog's neck.

Leather Buckle Collars

Limited-Slip Collar

Snap-Bolt Choke Collar

The martingale, Greyhound or limited-slip collar is preferred by many dog owners and trainers. It is fixed with an extra loop that tightens when pressure is applied to the leash. The martingale collar gets tighter but does not "choke" the dog. The limited-slip collar should only be used for walking and training, not for free play or interaction with another dog. These types of collar should never be left on the dog, as the extra loop can lead to accidents.

Choke collars, usually made of stainless steel, are made for training purposes but are not recommended for small dogs or heavily coated breeds. The chains can injure small dogs or damage long/abundant coats. Thin nylon choke leads are commonly used on show dogs while in the ring, though they are not practical for everyday use.

The harness, with two or three straps that attach over the dog's shoulders and around his torso, is a humane and safe alternative to the conventional collar. By and large, a well-made harness is virtually escape-proof. Harnesses are available in nylon and mesh and can be outfitted on most dogs ranging in chest girths of 10 to 30 inches.

Harness

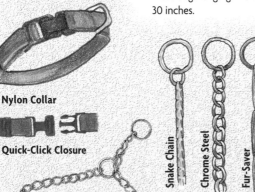

Nylon Collar

Quick-Click Closure

Snake Chain

Chrome Steel

Fur-Saver

Choke Chain Collars

A head collar, composed of a nylon strap that goes around the dog's muzzle and a second strap that wraps around his neck, offers the owner better control over his dog. This device is recommended for problem-solving with dogs (including jumping up, pulling and aggressive behaviors), but must be used with care.

A training halter, including a flat collar and two straps, made of nylon and webbing, is designed for walking. There are several on the market; some are more difficult to put on the dog than others. The halter harness, with two small slip rings at each end, is recommended for ease of use.

LEASHES

A 6-foot nylon lead is an excellent choice for a young puppy. It is lightweight and not as tempting to chew as a leather lead. You can switch to a 6-foot leather lead after your pup has grown and is used to walking politely on a lead. For initial puppy walks and house-training purposes, you should invest in a shorter lead so that you have more control over the puppy. At first, you don't want him wandering too far away from you, and when taking him out for toileting you will want to keep him in the specific area chosen for his potty spot.

Retractable leads are not recommended for Briards as they do not allow adequate control wth dogs as large as the Briard.

A Briard puppy will follow his nose everywhere he can. Be sure that you have puppy-proofed every inch of the interior (and exterior) of your home.

PET INSURANCE

Just as you can insure your car, your house and your own health, you likewise can insure your dog's health. Investigate a pet insurance policy by talking to your vet. Depending on the age of your dog, the breed and the kind of coverage you desire, your policy can be very affordable. Most policies cover accidental injuries, poisoning and thousands of medical problems and illnesses, including cancers. Some carriers also offer routine care and immunization coverage.

HOME SAFETY FOR YOUR PUPPY

The importance of puppy-proofing cannot be overstated. In addition to making your house comfortable for your Briard's arrival, you also must make sure that your house is safe for your puppy before you bring him home. There are countless hazards in the owner's personal living environment that a pup can sniff, chew, swallow or destroy. Many are obvious; others are not. Do a thorough advance house check to remove or rearrange those things that could hurt your puppy, keeping any potentially dangerous items out of areas to

LEASH LIFE

Dogs love leashes! Believe it or not, most dogs dance for joy every time their owners pick up their leashes. The leash means that the dog is going for a walk—and there are few things more exciting than that! Here are some of the kinds of leashes that are commercially available.

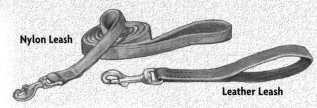

Nylon Leash

Leather Leash

Traditional Leash: Made of cotton, nylon or leather, these leashes are usually about 6 feet in length. A quality-made leather leash is softer on the hands than a nylon one. Durable woven cotton is a popular option. Lengths can vary up to about 48 feet, designed for different uses.

Chain Leash: Usually a metal chain leash with a plastic handle. This is not the best choice for most breeds, as it is heavier than other leashes and difficult to manage.

Retractable Leash: A long nylon cord is housed in a plastic device for extending and retracting. This leash, also known as a flexible leash, is ideal for taking trained dogs for long walks in open areas, although it is not always suitable for large, powerful breeds. Different lengths and sizes are available, so check that you purchase one appropriate for your dog's weight.

Elastic Leash: A nylon leash with an elastic extension. This is useful for well-trained dogs, especially in conjunction with a head halter.

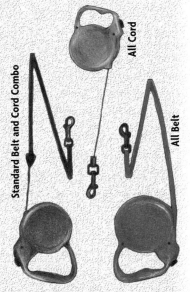

Standard Belt and Cord Combo

All Cord

All Belt

Retractable Leashes

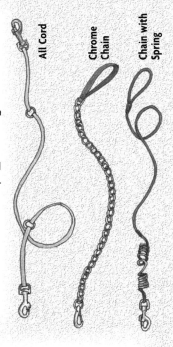

All Cord

Chrome Chain

Chain with Spring

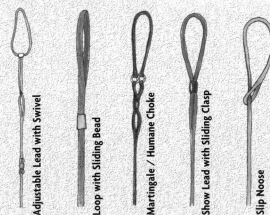

Adjustable Lead with Swivel

Loop with Sliding Bead

Martingale / Humane Choke

Show Lead with Sliding Clasp

Slip Noose

A Variety of Collar-Leash-in-One Products

Avoid leashes that are completely elastic, as they afford minimal control to the handler.

Adjustable Leash: This has two snaps, one on each end, and several metal rings. It is handy if you need to tether your dog temporarily, but is never to be used with a choke collar.

Tab Leash: A short leash (4 to 6 inches long) that attaches to your dog's collar. This device serves like a handle, in case you have to grab your dog while he's exercising off lead. It's ideal for "half-trained" dogs or dogs that listen only half of the time.

Slip Leash: Essentially a leash with a collar built in, similar to what a dog-show handler uses to show a dog. This British-style collar has a ring on the end so that you can form a slip collar. Useful if you have to catch your own runaway dog or a stray.

which he will have access. A Briard will quickly grow tall enough to take a drink from the toilet bowl, and garbage cans are also very popular with the breed.

Electrical cords are especially dangerous, since puppies view them as irresistible chew toys. Unplug and remove all exposed cords or fasten them beneath baseboards where the puppy cannot reach them. Veterinarians and firefighters can tell you horror stories about electrical burns and house fires that resulted from puppy-chewed electrical cords. Consider this a most serious precaution for your puppy and the rest of your family.

Scout your home for tiny objects that might be seen at a pup's eye level. Keep medication bottles and cleaning supplies well out of reach, and do the same with waste baskets and other trash containers. It goes without saying

ARE VACCINATIONS NECESSARY?

Vaccinations are recommended for all puppies by the American Veterinary Medical Association (AVMA). Some vaccines are absolutely necessary, while others depend upon a dog's or puppy's individual exposure to certain diseases or the animal's immune history. Rabies vaccinations are required by law in all 50 states. Some diseases are fatal whereas others are treatable, making the need for vaccinating against the latter questionable. Follow your veterinarian's recommendations to keep your dog fully immunized and protected. You can also review the AVMA directive on vaccinations on their website: www.avma.org.

that you should not use rodent poison or other toxic chemicals in any puppy area and that you must keep such containers safely locked up. You will be amazed at how many places a curious puppy can discover!

Once your house has cleared inspection, check your yard. A sturdy fence, well embedded into the ground, will give your dog a safe place to play and potty. Briards are large, athletic dogs, so a minimum 6-foot-high fence will be necessary to contain an agile youngster or adult. Check the fence periodically for necessary repairs. If there is a weak link or

Give the Briard safe toys to distract him from finding too much mischief when he is outdoors.

space to squeeze through, you can be sure a determined Briard will discover it.

The garage and shed can be hazardous places for a pup, as things like fertilizers, chemicals and tools are usually kept there. It's best to keep these areas off limits to the pup. Antifreeze is especially dangerous to dogs, as they find the taste appealing and it takes only a few licks from the driveway to kill a dog, puppy or adult, small breed or large.

VISITING THE VETERINARIAN

A good veterinarian is your Briard puppy's best health-insurance policy. If you do not already have a vet, ask friends and experienced dog people in your area for recommendations so that you can select a vet before you bring your Briard puppy home. Also arrange for your puppy's first veterinary examination beforehand, since many vets have two- and three-week waiting periods and your puppy should visit the vet within a day or so of coming home.

It's important to make sure your puppy's first visit to the vet is a pleasant and positive one. The vet should take great care to befriend the pup and handle him gently to make their first meeting a positive experience. The vet will give the pup a thorough physical examination and set up a schedule for vaccinations and other necessary wellness visits. Be sure to show your vet any health and inoculation records, which you should have received from your breeder. Your vet is a great source of canine health information, so be sure to ask questions and take notes. Creating a health journal for your puppy will make a handy reference for his wellness and any future health problems that may arise.

MEETING THE FAMILY

Your Briard's homecoming is an exciting time for all members of the family, and it's only natural that everyone will be eager to meet him, pet him and play with him. However, for the puppy's sake, it's best to make these initial family meetings as uneventful as possible so that the pup is not overwhelmed with too much too soon. Remember, he has just left his dam and his littermates and is away from the breeder's home for the first time. Despite his fuzzy wagging tail, he is still apprehensive and wondering where he is and who

Briards will sniff and search everything, so never leave anything potentially harmful for the snooping Briard.

THE CRITICAL SOCIALIZATION PERIOD

Canine research has shown that a puppy's 8th through 16th week is the most critical learning period of his life. This is when the puppy "learns to learn," a time when he needs positive experiences to build confidence and stability. Puppies who are not exposed to different people and situations outside the home during this period can grow up to be fearful and sometimes aggressive. This is also the best time for puppy lessons, since he has not yet acquired any bad habits that could undermine his ability to learn.

all these strange humans are. It's best to let him explore on his own and meet the family members as he feels comfortable. Let him investigate all the new smells, sights and sounds at his own pace. Children should be especially careful to not get overly excited, use loud voices or hug the pup too tightly. Be calm,

gentle and affectionate, and be ready to comfort him if he appears frightened or uneasy.

Be sure to show your puppy his new crate during this first day home. Toss a treat or two inside the crate; if he associates the crate with food, he will associate the crate with good things. If he is comfortable with the crate, you can offer him his first meal inside it. Leave the door ajar so he can wander in and out as he chooses.

FIRST NIGHT IN HIS NEW HOME

So much has happened in your Briard puppy's first day away from the breeder. He's had his first car ride to his new home. He's met his new human family and perhaps the other family pets. He has explored his new house and yard, at least those places where he is to be allowed during his first weeks at home. He may have visited his new veterinarian. He has eaten his first meal or two away from his dam and litter-mates. Surely that's enough to tire out an eight-week-old Briard pup—or so you hope!

It's bedtime. During the day, the pup investigated his crate, which is his new den and sleeping space, so it is not entirely strange to him. Line the crate with a soft towel or blanket that he can snuggle into and gently place him into the crate for the night. Some breeders send home a piece of bedding from where the pup slept with his littermates, and those familiar scents are a great comfort for the puppy on his first night without his siblings.

He will probably whine or cry. The puppy is objecting to the confinement and the fact that he is alone for the first time. This can be a stressful time for you as well as for the pup. It's important that you remain strong and don't let the puppy out of his crate to comfort him. He will fall asleep eventually. If you release him, the puppy will learn that crying means "out" and will continue that habit. You are laying the groundwork for future habits. Some breeders find that soft music can soothe a crying pup and help him get to sleep.

SOCIALIZING YOUR PUPPY

The first 20 weeks of your Briard puppy's life are the most important of his entire lifetime. A properly socialized puppy will grow up to be a confident and stable adult who will be a pleasure to live with and a welcome addition to the neighborhood.

The importance of socialization cannot be overemphasized. Research on canine behavior has proven that puppies who are not exposed to new sights, sounds, people and animals during their first 20 weeks of life will grow up to be timid and fearful, even aggressive, and unable to flourish outside of their home environment.

Socializing your puppy is not difficult and, in fact, will be a fun time for you both. Lead training goes hand in hand with socializa-

TEETHING TIME

All puppies chew. It's normal canine behavior. Chewing just plain feels good to a puppy, especially during the three- to five-month teething period when the adult teeth are breaking through the gums. Rather than attempting to eliminate such a strong natural chewing instinct, you will be more successful if you redirect it and teach your puppy what he may or may not chew. Correct inappropriate chewing with a sharp "No!" and offer him a chew toy, praising him when he takes it. Don't become discouraged. Chewing usually decreases after the adult teeth have come in.

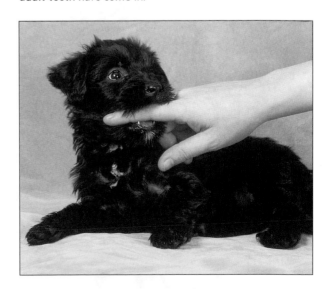

tion, so your puppy will be learning how to walk on a lead at the same time that he's meeting the neighborhood. Because the Briard is such a terrific breed, everyone will enjoy meeting "the new kid on the block." Take him for short walks to the park and to other dog-friendly places where he will encounter new people, especially children. Puppies automatically recognize children as "little people" and are drawn to play with them. Just make sure that you supervise these meetings and that the children do not get too rough or encourage him to play too hard. An overzealous pup can often nip too hard, frightening the child and in turn making the puppy overly excited. A bad experience in puppyhood can impact a dog for life, so a pup that has a negative experience with a child may grow up to be shy or even aggressive around children.

Take your puppy along on your daily errands. Puppies are natural "people magnets," and most people who see your pup will want to pet him. All of these encounters will help to mold him into a confident adult dog. Likewise, you will soon feel like a confident, responsible dog owner, rightly proud of your handsome Briard.

Be especially careful of your puppy's encounters and experiences during the eight- to ten-week-old period, which is also called the "fear period." This is a serious imprinting period, and all contact during this time should be gentle and positive. A frightening or negative event could leave a permanent impression that could affect his future behavior if a similar situation arises.

Also make sure that your puppy has received his first and second rounds of vaccinations before you expose him to other dogs or bring him to places that other dogs may frequent. Avoid dog parks and other strange-dog areas until your vet assures you that your puppy is fully immunized and resistant to the diseases that can be passed between canines. Discuss socialization with your breeder, as some breeders recommend socializing the puppy even before he has received all of his inoculations, depending on how outgoing the puppy may be.

LEADER OF THE PUPPY'S PACK
Like other canines, your puppy needs an authority figure, someone he can look up to and regard as the leader of his "pack." His first pack leader was his dam, who taught him to be polite and not chew too hard on her ears or nip at her muzzle. He learned those same lessons from his littermates. If he played too rough, they cried in pain and stopped the game, which sent an important message to the rowdy puppy.

Socialization of your Briard should be undertaken while he is still a puppy. He should meet other dogs and other people and become accustomed to traffic noises and walking on a lead.

As puppies play together, they are also struggling to determine who will be the boss. Being pack animals, dogs need someone to be in charge. If a litter of puppies remained together beyond puppyhood, one of the pups would emerge as the strongest one, the one who calls the shots.

Once your puppy leaves the pack, he will look intuitively for a new leader. If he does not recognize you as that leader, he will try to assume that position for himself. Of course, it is hard to imagine your adorable Briard puppy trying to be in charge when he is so small and seemingly helpless. You must remember that these are natural canine instincts. Do not cave in and allow your pup to get the upper "paw"!

Just as socialization is so important during these first 20 weeks, so too is your puppy's early education. He was born without

any bad habits. He does not know what is good or bad behavior. If he does things like nipping and digging, it's because he is having fun and doesn't know that humans consider these things as "bad." It's your job to teach him proper puppy manners, and this is the best time to accomplish that—before he has developed bad habits, since it is much more difficult to "unlearn" or correct unacceptable learned behavior than to teach good behavior from the start.

Make sure that all members of the family understand the importance of being consistent when training their new puppy. If you tell the puppy to stay off the sofa and your daughter allows him to cuddle on the couch to watch her favorite television show, your pup will be confused about what he is and is not allowed to do. Have a family conference before your pup comes home so that everyone

It will seem for the first few months that your Briard puppy's brains are in his mouth—all he can think about is chewing. Discourage the pup from chewing on your shoes, no matter how amusing you find it!

If you want to remain the head of your household, be consistent in letting your Briard puppy know what is and what is not acceptable behavior.

understands the basic principles of puppy training and the rules you have set forth for the pup and agrees to follow them.

The old saying that "an ounce of prevention is worth a pound of cure" is especially true when it comes to puppies. It is much easier to prevent inappropriate behavior than it is to change it. It's also easier and less stressful for the pup, since it will keep discipline to a minimum and create a more positive learning environment for him. That, in turn, will also be easier on you.

CHEWING AND NIPPING

Nipping at fingers and toes is normal puppy behavior. Chewing is also the way that puppies investigate their surroundings. However, you will have to teach your puppy that chewing anything other than his toys is not acceptable. That won't happen overnight and at times puppy teeth will test your patience. However, if you allow nipping and chewing to continue, just think about the damage that a mature Briard can do with a full set of adult teeth.

Whenever your puppy nips your hand or fingers, cry out "Ouch!" in a loud voice, which should startle your puppy and stop him from nipping, even if only for a moment. Immediately distract him by offering a small treat or an appropriate toy for him to chew instead (which means having chew toys and puppy treats handy or in your pockets at all times). Praise him when he takes the toy, and tell him what a good fellow he is. Praise is just as or even more important in puppy training as discipline and correction.

Puppies also tend to nip at children more often than adults, since they perceive little ones to be more vulnerable and more similar to their littermates. Teach your children appropriate responses to nipping behavior. If they are unable to handle it themselves, you may have to intervene. Puppy nips can be quite painful, and a child's frightened reaction will only encourage a puppy to nip harder, which is a natural canine response. As with all other puppy situations, interaction between your Briard puppy and children should be supervised.

Chewing on objects, not just family members' fingers and ankles, is also normal canine behavior that can be especially tedious (for the owner, not the pup) during the teething period when the puppy's adult teeth are coming in. At this stage, chewing just plain feels good. Furniture legs and cabinet corners are common puppy favorites. Shoes and other personal items also taste pretty good to a pup.

The best solution is, once again, prevention. If you value something, keep it tucked away and out of reach. You can't hide your dining-room table in a closet, but you can try to deflect the chewing by applying a bitter product made just to deter dogs from chewing. Available in a spray or cream, this substance is vile-tasting, although safe for dogs, and most puppies will avoid the forbidden object after one tiny taste. You also can apply the product to your leather leash if the puppy tries to chew on his lead during

KEEP OUT OF REACH

Most dogs don't browse around your medicine cabinet, but accidents do happen! The drug acetaminophen, the active ingredient in some over-the-counter pain relievers, can be deadly to dogs and cats if ingested in large quantities. Acetaminophen toxicity, caused by the dog's swallowing 15 to 20 tablets, can be manifested in abdominal pains within a day or two of ingestion, as well as liver damage. If you suspect your dog has swiped a bottle of medicine, get the dog to the vet immediately so that the vet can induce vomiting and cleanse the dog's stomach.

leash-training sessions.

Keep a ready supply of safe chews handy to offer your Briard as a distraction when he starts to chew on something that's a "no-no." Remember, at this tender age he does not yet know what is permitted or forbidden, so you have to be "on call" every minute he's awake and on the prowl.

You may lose a treasure or two during your puppy's growing-up period, and the furniture could sustain a nasty nick or two. These can be trying times, so be prepared for those inevitable accidents and comfort yourself in knowing that this too shall pass.

BRIARD

Adding a Briard to your household means adding a new family member who will need your care each and every day. When your Briard pup first comes home, you will start a routine with him so that, as he grows up, your dog will have a daily schedule just as you do. The aspects of your dog's daily care will likewise become regular parts of your day, so you'll both have a new schedule. Dogs learn by consistency and thrive on routine: regular times for meals, exercise, grooming and potty trips are just as important for your dog as they are for you! Your dog's schedule will depend much on your family's daily routine, but remember that you now have a new member of the family who is part of your day every day!

FEEDING

Feeding your dog the best diet is based on various factors, including age, activity level, overall condition and size of breed. When you visit the breeder, he will share with you his advice about the proper diet for your dog based on his experi-ence with the breed and the foods with which he has had success. Likewise, your vet will be a helpful source of advice throughout the dog's life and will aid you in planning a diet for optimal health.

FEEDING THE PUPPY

Of course, your pup's very first food will be his dam's milk. There may be special situations in which pups fail to nurse, necessitating that the breeder hand-feed them with a formula, but for the most part pups spend the first weeks of life nursing from their dam. The breeder weans the pups by gradually introducing solid foods and

TOXIC TREATS
Small amounts of fresh grapes and raisins can cause vomiting and diarrhea in dogs, possibly even kidney failure in the worst cases. Nuts, in general, are not recommended for dogs. Macadamia nuts, for example, can cause vomiting, diarrhea, fatigue and temporary paralysis of rear legs. Almonds are also especially problematic for dogs. Chocolate is one of the most lethal foods for dogs.

decreasing the milk meals. Pups may even start themselves off on the weaning process, albeit inadvertently, if they snatch bites from their mom's food bowl.

By the time the pups are ready for new homes, they are fully weaned and eating a good puppy food. As a new owner, you may be thinking, "Great! The breeder has taken care of the hard part." Not so fast.

A puppy's first year of life is the time when most of his growth and development takes place. This is a delicate time, especially for large-breed pups like the Briard, and diet plays a huge role in proper skeletal and muscular formation. Improper diet and exercise habits can lead to damaging problems that will compromise the dog's health and movement for his entire life. That being said, new owners should not worry needlessly. With the myriad types of food formulated specifically for growing pups of different-sized breeds, dog-food manufacturers have taken much of the guesswork out of feeding your puppy well. Since growth-food formulas are designed to provide the nutrition that a growing puppy needs, it is unnecessary and, in fact, can prove harmful to add supplements to the diet. Research has shown that too much of certain vitamin supplements and minerals predispose a dog to

Feeding the adult Briard will not present a challenge to the owner once a suitable high-quality dry food is selected.

skeletal problems. It's by no means a case of "if a little is good, a lot is better." At every stage of your dog's life, too much or too little in the way of nutrients can be harmful, which is why a manufactured complete food is the easiest way to know that your dog is getting what he needs.

Because of a young pup's small body and accordingly small digestive system, his daily portion will be divided up into small meals throughout the day. This can mean starting off with three or more meals a day and decreasing the number of meals as the pup matures. For the adult, dividing the day's food into two meals on a morning/evening schedule is healthier for the dog's digestion than one large daily portion.

Regarding the feeding

schedule, feeding the pup at the same times and in the same place each day is important for both housebreaking purposes and establishing the dog's everyday routine. As for the amount to feed, growing puppies generally need proportionately more food per body weight than their adult counterparts, but a pup should never be allowed to gain excess weight. Dogs of all ages should be kept in proper body condition, but extra weight can strain a pup's developing frame, causing skeletal problems.

Watch your pup's weight as he grows and, if the recommended amounts seem to be too much or too little for your pup, consult the vet about appropriate dietary changes. Keep in mind that treats, although small, can quickly add up throughout the day, contributing unnecessary calories. Treats are fine when used prudently; opt for dog treats specially formulated to be healthy or for nutritious snacks like small pieces of cheese or cooked chicken.

FEEDING THE ADULT DOG

For the adult (meaning physically mature) dog, feeding properly is about maintenance, not growth. Again, correct weight is a concern. Your dog should appear fit and should have an evident "waist." His ribs should not be protruding (a sign of being underweight), but they should be covered by only a slight layer of fat. Under normal circumstances, an adult dog can be maintained fairly easily with a high-quality nutritionally complete adult-formula food.

Factor treats into your dog's overall daily caloric intake and avoid offering table scraps. Overweight dogs are more prone to health problems. Research has even shown that obesity takes years off a dog's life. With that in mind, resist the urge to overfeed and over-treat. Don't make unnecessary additions to your dog's diet, whether with tidbits or with extra vitamins and minerals.

BLOAT PREVENTATIVE

Gastric torsion, or bloat, is a killer of Briards, and the research does link its incidence to the diet fed. Never feed cheap grain-based food, as this swells greatly in the stomach and is dangerous. Before feeding a dry dog food to your Briard, test one piece in a glass of water; many manufacturers offer small free samples. If the bit of food swells, do not buy it. If after soaking for half an hour or so it is the same size, then it is suitable to offer to your Briard. Whatever happens in the water glass mirrors what will happen in the dog's stomach when filled with digestive acid.

The amount of food needed for proper maintenance will vary depending on the individual dog's activity level, but you will be able to tell whether the daily portions are keeping him in good shape. With the wide variety of good complete foods available, choosing what to feed is largely a matter of personal preference. Just as with the puppy, the adult dog should have consistency in his mealtimes and feeding place. In addition to a consistent routine, regular mealtimes enable the owner to practice important bloat preventives and allow the owner to see how much his dog is eating. If the dog seems never to be satisfied or, likewise, becomes uninterested in his food, the owner will know right away that something is wrong and can consult the vet.

DIETS FOR THE AGING DOG

A good rule of thumb is that once a dog has reached 75% of his expected lifespan, he has reached "senior citizen" or geriatric status. Your Briard will be considered a senior at about 8 years of age; based on his size, he has a projected lifespan of about 11 years. (The smallest breeds generally enjoy the longest lives and the largest breeds the shortest.)

What does aging have to do with your dog's diet? No, he won't get a discount at the local

diner's early-bird special. Yes, he will require some dietary changes to accommodate the changes that come along with increased age. One change is that the older dog's dietary needs become more similar to that of a puppy. Specifically, dogs can metabolize more protein as youngsters and seniors than in the adult-mainte-nance stage. Discuss with your vet whether you need to switch to a higher-protein or senior-formulated food or whether your current adult-dog food contains sufficient nutrition for the senior.

Watching the dog's weight remains essential, even more so in the senior stage. Older dogs are already more vulnerable to illness, and obesity only contributes to their susceptibility to problems. As the older dog becomes less active and, thus exercises less, his regular portions may cause him to gain weight. At this point, you may consider decreasing his daily food intake or switching to a reduced-calorie food. As with other changes, you should consult your vet for advice.

Stainless steel food and water bowls are the best bet for your Briard, as he is less inclined to chew on them.

HOLD THE ONIONS

Sliced, chopped, grated; dehydrated, boiled, fried or raw; pearl, Spanish, white or red: onions can be deadly to your dog. The toxic effects of onions in dogs are cumulative for up to 30 days. A serious form of anemia, called Heinz body anemia, affects the red blood cells of dogs that have eaten onions. For safety (and better breath), dogs should avoid chives and scallions as well.

TYPES OF FOOD AND READING THE LABEL

When selecting the type of food to feed your dog, it is important to check out the label for ingredients. Many dry-food products have soybean, corn or rice as the main ingredient. The main ingredient will be listed first on the label, with the rest of the ingredients following in descending order according to their proportion in the food. While these types of dry food are fine, you should also look into dry foods based on meat or fish. These are better-quality foods and thus higher priced. However, they may be just as economical in the long run because studies have shown that it takes less of the higher-quality foods to maintain a dog.

Comparing the various types of food, dry, canned and semi-moist, dry foods contain the least amount of water and canned foods the most. Proportionately, dry foods are the most calorie- and nutrient-dense, which means that you need more of a canned food product to supply the same amount of nutrition. In households domiciling breeds of disparate sizes, the canned/dry/semi-moist question can be of special importance. Larger breeds obviously eat more than smaller ones and thus in general do better on dry foods, but smaller breeds do fine on canned foods and require "small bite" formulations to protect their small mouths and teeth if fed only dry foods. So if you have breeds of different size in your household, consider both your own preferences and what your dogs like to eat, but mainly think canned for the little guys and dry or semi-moist for everyone else. You may find success mixing the food types as well. Water is important for all dogs, but even more so for those fed dry foods, as there is no high water content in their food.

There are strict controls that regulate the nutritional content of dog food, and a food has to meet the minimum requirements in order to be considered "complete and balanced." It is important that you choose such a food for your dog, so check the label to be sure that your chosen food meets the requirements. If not, look for a food that clearly states on the

What Is "Bloat" and How Do I Prevent it?

We have mentioned the term "bloat," which refers to gastric torsion (gastric dilatation/volvulus), a potentially fatal condition. As it is directly related to feeding and exercise practices, a brief explanation here is warranted. The term *dilatation* means that the dog's stomach is filled with air, while *volvulus* means that the stomach is twisted around on itself, blocking the entrance/exit points. Dilatation/volvulus is truly a deadly combination, although they also can occur independently of each other. An affected dog cannot digest food or pass gas, and blood cannot flow to the stomach, causing accumulation of toxins and gas along with great pain and rapidly occuring shock.

Many theories exist on what exactly causes bloat, but we do know that deep-chested breeds like the Briard are more prone. Activities like eating a large meal, gulping water, strenuous exercise too close to mealtimes or a combination of these factors can contribute to bloat, though not every case is directly related to these more well-known causes. With that in mind, we can focus on incorporating simple daily preventives and knowing how to recognize the symptoms. In addition to the tips presented in this book, ask your vet about how to prevent and recognize bloat. An affected dog needs immediate veterinary attention, as death can result quickly. Signs include obvious restlessness/discomfort, crying in pain, drooling/excessive salivation, unproductive attempts to vomit or relieve himself, visibly bloated appearance and collapsing. Do not wait: get to the vet *right away* if you see any of these symptoms. The vet will confirm by x-ray if the stomach is bloated with air; if so, the dog must be treated *immediately*.

As varied as the causes of bloat are the tips for prevention, but some common preventive methods follow:
• Feed two or three small meals daily rather than one large one;
• Do not feed water before, after or with meals, but allow access to water at all other times;
• Never permit rapid eating or gulping of water;
• No exercise for the dog at least two hours before and (especially) after meals;
• Feed high-quality food with adequate protein, adequate fiber content and not too much fat and carbohydrate;
• Explore herbal additives, enzymes or gas-reduction products (only under a vet's advice) to encourage a "friendly" environment in the dog's digestive system;
• Avoid foods and ingredients known to produce gas;
• Avoid stressful situations for the dog, especially at mealtimes;
• Make dietary changes gradually, over a period of a few weeks;
• Do not feed dry food only;
• Although the role of genetics as a causative of bloat is not known, many breeders do not breed from previously affected dogs;
• Sometimes owners are advised to have gastroplexy (stomach stapling) performed on their dogs as a preventive measure;
• Pay attention to your dog's behavior and any changes that could be symptomatic of bloat. Your dog's life depends on it!

Fresh drinking water is an important component of your Briard's diet and good health.

label that it is formulated to be complete and balanced for your dog's particular stage of life.

Recommendations for amounts to feed will also be indicated on the label. You should also ask your vet about proper food portions, and you will keep an eye on your dog's condition to see whether the recommended amounts are adequate. If he becomes over- or underweight, you will need to make adjustments; this also would be a good time to consult your vet.

The food label may also make feeding suggestions, such as whether moistening a dry-food product is recommended. Sometimes a splash of water will help the dog to eat more slowly and even enhance the flavor. Don't be overwhelmed by the

many factors that go into feeding your dog. Manufacturers of complete and balanced foods make it easy, and once you find the right food and amounts for your Briard, his daily feeding will be a matter of routine.

DON'T FORGET THE WATER!
For a dog, it's always time for a drink! Regardless of what type of food he eats, there's no doubt that he needs plenty of water. Fresh cold water, in a clean bowl, should be freely available to your dog at all times. There are special circumstances, such as during puppy housebreaking, when you will want to monitor your pup's water intake so that you will be able to predict when he will need to relieve himself, but water must be available to him nonetheless. Water is essential for hydration and proper body function just as it is in humans.

You will get to know how much your dog typically drinks in a day. Of course, in the heat or if exercising vigorously, he will be more thirsty and will drink more. However, if he begins to drink noticeably more water for no apparent reason, this could signal any of various problems, and you are advised to consult your vet.

Water is the best drink for dogs. Some owners are tempted to give milk from time to time or to moisten dry food with milk, but dogs do not have the enzymes necessary to digest the lactose in milk, which is much different from the milk that nursing puppies receive. Therefore stick with clean, fresh water to quench your dog's thirst, and always have it readily available to him.

A word of caution concerning your deep-chested dog's water intake: he should never be allowed to gulp water, especially at mealtimes. In fact, his water intake should be restricted at mealtimes as a rule. This simple daily precaution can go a long way in protecting your dog from the dangerous and potentially fatal gastric torsion (bloat).

EXERCISE

PUPPIES
A Briard has quite a bit of growing to do going from puppyhood to adulthood. Most of this seems to be done when the puppy is sleeping, and sleep and rest are vital to the growing puppy. Exercise should be limited and gentle when your Briard is small, but once his leg bones have finished growing, at roughly a year of age, your Briard is able to manage much more exercise. The last bones to stop growing are the skull bones, but this does not have a bearing on the exercise regimen you create for your dog.

TWO'S COMPANY
One surefire method of increasing your adult dog's exercise plan is to adopt a second dog. If your dog is well socialized, he should take to his new canine pal in no time and soon the two will be giving each other lots of activity and exercise as they play, romp and explore together. Most owners agree that two dogs are hardly much more work than one. If you cannot afford a second dog, get together with a friend or neighbor who has a well-trained dog. Your dog will definitely enjoy the company of a new four-legged playmate.

ADULT DOGS
Although an adult Briard is large, he does not need miles and miles of walking daily. However, a sedentary lifestyle is as harmful to a dog as it is to a person. Regular walks, play sessions in the yard or letting the adult dog run free in the securely fenced yard under supervision are the

For the first year of your Briard's life, the puppy should be able to get sufficient exercise from roaming around your fenced yard.

best forms of exercise. Getting into a routine of a daily lengthy walk, no matter what the weather, is the best way to keep your Briard at his fittest. If you have a "couch potato," increase the exercise slowly. Not only is exercise essential to keep the dog's body fit, it is essential to his mental well-being as well. A bored dog will find something to do, which often manifests itself in some type of destructive behavior. In this sense, it is essential for the owner's mental well-being as well.

GROOMING

Your Briard will need to be groomed regularly, so it is essential that brief grooming sessions are introduced at a very early age. From the very beginning, a few minutes each day should be set aside for grooming. Increase the duration of the sessions, building up slowly as the puppy matures and the coat grows in length. Though a puppy is initially quite small, and small dogs are usually groomed on tables, it is not long until the gangly adolescent is far too big to be put on a table safely.

Start brushing by introducing a few gentle brush strokes. Be sure not to tug at any knots at this stage, for this would cause the puppy to associate grooming with pain. This may take a little getting used to for both you and your puppy. Not only does the coat get longer with age, allowing more tangles to form behind the ears and elbows and in the trousers, but also the coat will change from the fluffier puppy coat to the silkier adult one.

A grooming table makes the chore of grooming the Briard's coat more manageable. Since the Briard is such a large dog, with an abundant coat, grooming is a time-consuming venture.

You will certainly need to groom the coat between bath times, and it is best to moisten it with either a spray of water or a light conditioning spray before you begin grooming.

ROUTINE GROOMING

Initially the coat should be brushed section by section in the direction of coat growth. It is imperative to groom right down to the skin so that the undercoat is not left matted. The best brush to use is a good-quality bristle brush; a better-quality brush will cost more money but will generally do a better job.

If you do find a mat in the coat, spray the mat with a generous amount of conditioning or anti-tangle spray. Leave this to soak in for a few moments, then gently tease out the mat with your fingers. Always work from the inside out or the knot will just get tighter! Be careful not to tug at the knot—it will be painful for the pup and will also pull out too much coat.

Take care in grooming the tummy and under the "armpits," for these areas are especially sensitive. There is really no harm in cutting away small tight knots from under the armpits, as these will not show and the dog will feel more comfortable. However, a Briard in show coat should not be trimmed, so scissors should only be used when absolutely

You must be diligent in grooming your Briard to keep him looking his best. Regular brushing will help maintain an attractive coat.

necessary. Trimming below the pads of the feet prevents uncomfortable hairballs from forming between the pads. Another area that will need special attention is the hair behind the ears. This hair is often of a softer texture and knots easily.

The trousers of a Briard are heavily coated and will also need regular grooming. To prevent knots and tangles, be sure to remove any debris that may have accumulated following a visit outdoors. Also, always check your dog's back end to see that nothing remains attached to the coat from his relieving himself. Between baths you may like to use a damp sponge, but always be sure to dry the coat thoroughly. Drying will help to keep the dog comfortable.

Make checking the eyes, ears and feet part of the regular

WATER SHORTAGE

No matter how well behaved your dog is, bathing is always a project! Nothing can substitute for a good warm bath, but owners do have the option of giving their dogs "dry" baths. Pet shops sell excellent products, in both powder and spray forms, designed for spot-cleaning your dog. These dry shampoos are convenient for touch-up jobs when you don't have the time to bathe your dog in the traditional way.

Muddy feet, messy behinds and smelly coats can be spot-cleaned and deodorized with a "wet-nap"-style cleaner. On those days when your dog insists on rolling in fresh goose droppings and there's no time for a bath, a spot bath can save the day. These pre-moistened wipes are also handy for other grooming needs like wiping faces, ears and eyes and freshening tails and behinds.

grooming routine. If needed, the eyes can be cleaned using a canine liquid eye cleaner; a special cleaner is also available for cleaning the ears. Pay attention to the feet; be sure you don't allow knots to build up between the toes, and always keep an eye on the length of the toenails.

BATHING

In general, dogs need to be bathed only a few times a year, possibly more often if your dog gets into something messy or if he starts to smell like a dog. Show dogs are usually bathed before every show, which could be as frequent as weekly, although this depends on the owner. Bathing too frequently can have negative effects on the skin and coat, removing natural oils and causing dryness.

If you give your dog his first bath when he is young, he will become accustomed to the process. Wrestling a dog into the tub or chasing a freshly shampooed dog who has escaped from the bath will be no fun. Most dogs don't naturally enjoy their baths, but you at least want yours to cooperate with you.

Before bathing the dog, have the items you'll need close at hand. First, decide where you will bathe the dog. You should have a tub or basin with a non-slip surface. Puppies can even be bathed in a sink. In warm weather, some like to use a portable pool in the yard, although you'll want to make sure your dog doesn't head for the nearest dirt pile following his bath! You will also need a hose or shower spray to wet the coat thoroughly, a shampoo formulated for dogs, absorbent towels and a blow dryer. Human shampoos are too harsh for dogs' coats and will dry them out.

Before wetting the dog, give

him a brush-through to remove any dead hair, dirt and mats. Make sure he is at ease in the tub and have the water at a comfortable temperature. Begin bathing by wetting the coat all the way down to the skin. Massage in the shampoo, keeping it away from his face and eyes and being careful not to create knots. Rinse him thoroughly, again avoiding the eyes and ears, as you don't want to get water into the ear canals. A thorough rinsing is important, as shampoo residue is drying and itchy to the dog. After rinsing, wrap him in a towel to absorb the initial moisture. You can then finish drying with a blow dryer on low heat, held at a safe distance from the dog and brushing the coat as you go. Introduce the blow dryer when your Briard is a pup so that he gets used to the noise. You should keep the dog indoors and away from drafts until he is completely dry.

NAIL CLIPPING
Having their nails trimmed is not on many dogs' lists of favorite things to do. With this in mind, you will need to accustom your puppy to the procedure at a young age so that he will sit still (well, as still as he can) for his pedicures. Long nails can cause the dog's feet to spread, which is not good for him; likewise, long nails can hurt if they unintentionally scratch, not good for you.

Some dogs' nails are worn down naturally by regular walking on hard surfaces, so the frequency with which you clip depends on your individual dog. Look at his nails from time to time and clip as needed; a good way to know when it's time for a trim is if you hear your dog clicking as he walks across the floor.

There are several types of nail clippers and even electric nail-grinding tools made for dogs; first we'll discuss using the clipper. To start, have your clipper ready and some doggie treats on hand. You want your pup to view his nail-clipping sessions in a positive light, and what better way to convince him than with food? You may want to enlist the help of an assistant to

If you accustom your Briard to nail clipping as a puppy, you'll have little trouble giving him a pedicure later in life.

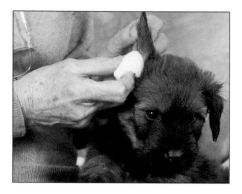

Keep your dog's ears clean with a piece of cotton and a cleaner available from your vet or pet store.

comfort the pup and offer treats as you concentrate on the clipping itself. The guillotine-type clipper is thought of by many as the easiest type to use; the nail tip is inserted into the opening, and blades on the top and bottom snip it off in one clip.

Start by grasping the pup's paw; a little pressure on the foot pad causes the nail to extend, making it easier to clip. Clip off a little at a time. If you can see the "quick," which is a blood vessel that runs through each nail, you will know how much to trim, as you do not want to cut into the quick. On that note, if you do cut the quick, which will cause bleeding, you can stem the flow of blood with a styptic pencil or other clotting agent. If you mistakenly nip the quick, do not panic or fuss, as this will cause the pup to be afraid. Simply reassure the pup, stop the bleeding and move on to the next nail. Don't be discouraged; you

will become a professional canine pedicurist with practice.

You may or may not be able to see the quick, so it's best to just clip off a small bit at a time. If you see a dark dot in the center of the nail, this is the quick and your cue to stop clipping. Tell the puppy he's a "good boy" and offer a piece of treat with each nail. You can also use nail-clipping time to examine the footpads, making sure that they are not dry and cracked and that nothing has become embedded in them.

The nail grinder, the other choice, is many owners' first choice. Accustoming the puppy to the sound of the grinder and sensation of the buzz presents fewer challenges than the clipper, and there's no chance of cutting through the quick. Use the grinder on a low setting and always talk soothingly to your dog. He won't mind his salon visit, and he'll have nicely polished nails as well.

EAR CLEANING

While keeping your dog's ears clean unfortunately will not cause him to "hear" your commands any better, it will protect him from ear infection and ear-mite infestation. In addition, a dog's ears are vulnerable to waxy build-up and to collecting foreign matter from the outdoors. Look in your dog's ears regularly to ensure that they look pink, clean and otherwise healthy. Even if they look fine, an odor in the ears signals a problem and means it's time to call the vet.

A dog's ears should be cleaned regularly; once a week is suggested, and you can do this along with your regular brushing. Using a cotton ball or pad, and never probing into the ear canal, wipe the ear gently. You can use an ear-cleansing liquid or powder available from your vet or pet-supply store; alternatively, you might prefer to use homemade solutions with ingredients like one part white vinegar and one part hydrogen peroxide. Ask your vet about home remedies before you attempt to concoct something on your own!

Keep your dog's ears free of excess hair by plucking it as needed. If done gently, this will be painless for the dog. Look for wax, brown droppings (a sign of ear mites), redness or any other abnormalities. At the first sign of a problem, contact your vet so that he can prescribe an appropriate medication.

EYE CARE
During grooming sessions, pay extra attention to the condition of your dog's eyes. If the area around the eyes is soiled or if tear staining has occurred, there are various cleaning agents made especially for this purpose. Look at the dog's eyes to make sure no debris has entered; dogs with large eyes and those who spend time

Owning a Briard (or two) requires that you have a suitable vehicle to travel with the dog(s). Crates and special divider gates make traveling convenient and safe for Briards and owners alike.

outdoors are especially prone to this.

The signs of an eye infection are obvious: mucus, redness, puffiness, scabs or other signs of irritation. If your dog's eyes become infected, the vet will likely prescribe an antibiotic ointment for treatment. If you notice signs of more serious problems, such as opacities in the eye, which usually indicate cataracts, consult the vet at once.

ID FOR YOUR DOG

You love your Briard and want to keep him safe. Of course you take every precaution to prevent his escaping from the yard or becoming lost or stolen. You have a sturdy high fence and you always keep your dog on lead when out and about in public places. If your dog is not properly identified, however, you are overlooking a major aspect of his safety. We hope to never be in a situation where our dog is missing, but we should practice prevention in the unfortunate case that this happens; identification greatly increases the chances of your dog's being returned to you.

There are several ways to identify your dog. First, the traditional dog tag should be a staple in your dog's wardrobe, attached to his everyday collar. Tags can be made of sturdy plastic and various metals and should include your contact information so that a person who finds the dog can get in touch with you right away to arrange his return. Many people today enjoy the wide range of decorative tags available, so have fun and create a tag to match your dog's personality. It is important that the tag stays on the collar, so have a secure "O" ring attachment; you also can explore the type of tag that slides right onto the collar.

In addition to the ID tag, which every dog should wear even if identified by another method, two other forms of identification have become popular: microchipping and tattooing. In microchipping, a tiny scannable chip is painlessly inserted under the dog's skin. The number is registered to you so that, if your lost dog turns up at a clinic or shelter, the chip can be scanned to retrieve your contact information.

The advantage of the microchip is that it is a permanent form of ID, but there are some factors to consider. Several different companies make microchips, and not all are compatible with the others' scanning devices. It's best to find a company with a universal microchip that can be read by scanners made by other companies as well. It won't do any good to have the dog chipped if the information cannot be retrieved. Also, not every humane society, shelter and clinic is equipped with a scanner, although more and more facilities are equipping themselves. In fact, many shelters microchip dogs that they adopt out to new homes.

Because the microchip is not visible to the eye, the dog must wear a tag that states that he is microchipped so that whoever picks him up will know to have him scanned. He of course also should have a tag with contact information in case his chip cannot be read. Humane societies and veterinary clinics offer this service, which is usually very affordable.

Though less popular than microchipping, tattooing is another permanent method of identification for dogs. Most vets perform this service, and there are also clinics that perform dog tattooing. This is also an affordable procedure and one that will not cause much discomfort for the dog. It is best to put the tattoo in a visible area, such as the ear, to deter theft. It is sad to say that there are cases of dogs' being stolen and sold to research laboratories, but such laboratories will not accept tattooed dogs.

To ensure that the tattoo is effective in aiding your dog's return to you, the tattoo number must be registered with a national organization. That way, when someone finds a tattooed dog, a phone call to the registry will quickly match the dog with his owner.

Select a top-rate boarding kennel well before you actually need one. Be sure it is clean and properly staffed and that it offers its doggie guests regular exercise and attention.

BASIC TRAINING PRINCIPLES: PUPPY VS. ADULT

There's a big difference between training an adult dog and training a young puppy. With a young puppy, everything is new. At eight to ten weeks of age, he will be experiencing many things, and he has nothing with which to compare these experiences. Up to this point, he has been with his dam and littermates, not one-on-one with people except in his interactions with his breeder and visitors to the litter.

When you first bring the puppy home, he is eager to please you. This means that he accepts doing things your way. During the next couple of months, he will absorb the basis of everything he needs to know for the rest of his

More so than other breeds of dog, the herding dogs follow their master's instructions and can make decisions of their own.

life. This early age is even referred to as the "sponge" stage. After that, for the next 18 months, it's up to you to reinforce good manners by building on the foundation that you've established. Once your puppy is reliable in basic commands and behavior and has reached the appropriate age, you may gradually introduce him to some of the interesting sports, games and activities available to pet owners and their dogs.

Raising your puppy is a family affair. Each member of the family must know what rules to set forth for the puppy and how to use the same one-word commands to mean exactly the same thing every time. Even if yours is a large family, one person will soon be considered by the pup to be the leader, the alpha person in his pack, the "boss" who must be obeyed. Often that highly regarded person turns out to be the one who feeds the puppy. Food ranks very high on the puppy's list of important things! That's why your puppy is rewarded with small treats along with verbal praise when he responds to you correctly. As the puppy learns to do what you want him to do, the food rewards are gradually eliminated and only the praise remains. If you were to keep up with the food treats, you could have two problems on your hands—an obese dog and a beggar.

You will need to have your Briard's complete attention whenever he undergoes any training. Adult dogs are more difficult to train, but, if the owner places emphasis on follow-through for all commands, success is usually met.

Training begins the minute your Briard puppy steps through the doorway of your home, so don't make the mistake of putting the puppy on the floor and telling him by your actions to "Go for it! Run wild!" Even if this is your first puppy, you must act as if you know what you're doing: be the boss. An uncertain pup may be terrified to move, while a bold one will be ready to take you at your word and start plotting to destroy the house! Before you collected your puppy, you decided where his own special place would be, and that's where to put him when you first arrive home. Give him a house tour after he has investigated his area and had a nap and a bathroom "pit stop."

It's worth mentioning here that if you've adopted an adult dog that is completely trained to your liking, lucky you! You're off the hook! However, if that dog spent his life up to this point in a kennel, or even in a good home but without any real training, be prepared to tackle the job ahead. A dog three years of age or older with no previous training cannot be blamed for not knowing what he was never taught. While the dog is trying to understand and learn your rules, at the same time he has to unlearn many of his previously self-taught habits and general view of the world.

Working with a professional trainer will speed up your progress with an adopted adult dog. You'll need patience, too. Some new rules may be close to impossible for the dog to accept. After all, he's been successful so far by doing everything his way! (Patience again.) He may agree with your instruction for a few days and then slip back into his old ways, so you must be just as consistent and understanding in your teaching as you would be with a puppy. (More patience needed yet again!) Your dog has to learn to pay attention to your voice, your family, the daily routine, new smells, new sounds and, in some cases, even a new climate.

One of the most important things to find out about a newly adopted adult dog is his reaction to children (yours and others), strangers and your friends and how he acts upon meeting other dogs. If he was not socialized with dogs as a puppy, this could be a major problem. This does not mean that he's a "bad" dog, a vicious dog or an aggressive dog; rather, it means that he has no idea how to read another dog's body language. There's no way for him to tell whether the other dog is a friend or foe. Survival instinct takes over, telling him to attack first and ask questions later. This definitely calls for professional help and, even then, may not be a behavior that can be corrected 100% reliably (or even at all). If you have a puppy, this is why it is so very important to introduce your young puppy properly to other puppies and "dog-friendly" adult dogs.

HOUSE-TRAINING YOUR BRIARD

Dogs are tactility-oriented when it comes to house-training. In other words, they respond to the surface on which they are given approval to eliminate. The choice is yours (the dog's version is in parentheses): The lawn (including the neighbors' lawns)? A bare patch of earth under a tree (where people like to sit and relax in the summertime)? Concrete steps or patio (all sidewalks, garages and basement floors)? The curbside (watch out for cars)? A small area

Canine Development Schedule

It is important to understand how and at what age a puppy develops into adulthood.
If you are a puppy owner, consult this Canine Development Schedule to
determine the stage of development your puppy is currently experiencing.
This knowledge will help you as you work with the puppy in the weeks and months ahead.

Period	Age	Characteristics
First to Third	Birth to Seven Weeks	Puppy needs food, sleep and warmth and responds to simple and gentle touching. Needs mother for security and disciplining. Needs littermates for learning and interacting with other dogs. Pup learns to function within a pack and learns pack order of dominance. Begin socializing pup with adults and children for short periods. Pup begins to become aware of his environment.
Fourth	Eight to Twelve Weeks	Brain is fully developed. Pup needs socializing with outside world. Remove from mother and littermates. Needs to change from canine pack to human pack. Human dominance necessary. Fear period occurs between 8 and 12 weeks. Avoid fright and pain.
Fifth	Thirteen to Sixteen Weeks	Training and formal obedience should begin. Less association with other dogs, more with people, places, situations. Period will pass easily if you remember this is pup's change-to-adolescence time. Be firm and fair. Flight instinct prominent. Permissiveness and over-disciplining can do permanent damage. Praise for good behavior.
Juvenile	Four to Eight Months	Another fear period about seven to eight months of age. It passes quickly, but be cautious of fright and pain. Sexual maturity reached. Dominant traits established. Dog should understand sit, down, come and stay by now.

NOTE: THESE ARE APPROXIMATE TIME FRAMES. ALLOW FOR INDIVIDUAL DIFFERENCES IN PUPPIES.

of crushed stone in a corner of the yard (mine!)? The latter is the best choice if you can manage it, because it will remain strictly for the dog's use and is easy to keep clean.

You can start out with paper-training indoors and switch over to an outdoor surface as the puppy matures and gains control over his need to eliminate. For the naysayers, don't worry—this won't mean that the dog will soil on every piece of newspaper lying around the house. You are training him to go outside, remember? Starting out by paper-training often is the only choice for a city dog.

WHEN YOUR PUPPY'S "GOT TO GO"

Your puppy's need to relieve himself is seemingly non-stop, but signs of improvement will be seen each week. From 8 to 10 weeks old, the puppy will have to be taken outside every time he wakes up, about 10–15 minutes after every meal and after every period of play—all day long, from first thing in the morning until his bedtime! That's a total of ten or more trips per day to teach the puppy where it's okay to relieve himself. With that schedule in mind, you can see that house-training a young puppy is not a part-time job. It requires someone to be home all day.

If that seems overwhelming or impossible, do a little planning.

For example, plan to pick up your puppy at the start of a vacation period. If you can't get home in the middle of the day, plan to hire a dog-sitter or ask a neighbor to come over to take the pup outside, feed him his lunch and then take him out again about ten or so minutes after he's eaten. Also make arrangements with that or another person to be your "emergency" contact if you have to stay late on the job. Remind yourself—repeatedly—that this hectic schedule improves as the puppy gets older.

HOME WITHIN A HOME

Your Briard puppy needs to be confined to one secure, puppy-proof area when no one is able to watch his every move. Generally the kitchen is the place of choice because the floor is washable. Likewise, it's a busy family area that will accustom the pup to a variety of noises, everything from pots and pans to the telephone, blender and dishwasher. He will also be enchanted by the smell of your cooking (and will never be critical when you burn something). A sturdy exercise pen (also called an "ex-pen") within the room of choice is an excellent means of confinement for a young pup as long as he cannot climb out. He can see out and has a certain amount of space in which to run about, but he is safe from dangerous things like electrical cords, heating units, trash baskets or open kitchen-supply cabinets. Place the pen where the puppy will not get a blast of heat or air conditioning.

In the pen, you can put a few safe toys, his bed (which can be his crate if the dimensions of pen and crate are compatible) and a few layers of newspaper in one small corner, just in case. A water bowl can be hung at a convenient height on the side of the ex-pen so it won't become a splashing pool for an innovative puppy. His food dish can go on the floor, next to but not under the water bowl.

Crates are something that pet owners are at last getting used to for their dogs. Wild or domestic canines have always preferred to sleep in den-like safe spots, and that is exactly what the crate provides. How often have you seen adult dogs that choose to sleep under a table or chair even though they have full run of the house? It's the den connection.

In your "happy" voice, use the word "Crate" every time you put the pup into his den. If he's new to a crate, toss in a small biscuit for him to chase the first few times. At night, after he's been outside, he should sleep in his crate. The crate may be kept in his designated area at night or, if you want to be sure to hear those wake-up yips in the morning, put the crate in a corner of your bedroom. However, don't make

CREATURES OF HABIT

Canine behaviorists and trainers aptly describe dogs as "creatures of habit," meaning that dogs respond to structure in their daily lives and welcome a routine. Do not interpret this to mean that dogs enjoy endless repetition in their training sessions. Dogs get bored just as humans do. Keep training sessions interesting and exciting. Vary the commands and the locations in which you practice. Give short breaks for play in between lessons. A bored student will never be the best performer in the class.

any response whatsoever to whining or crying. If he's completely ignored, he'll settle down and get to sleep.

Good bedding for a young puppy is an old folded bath towel or an old blanket, something that is easily washable and disposable if necessary ("accidents" will happen!). Never put newspaper in the puppy's crate. Also those old ideas about adding a clock to replace his mother's heartbeat or a

Paper-training is only feasible with very young Briards due to the breed's large size. It is preferable to train the Briard pup to the outdoors from the beginning.

hot-water bottle to replace her warmth, are just that—old ideas. The clock could drive the puppy nuts, and the hot-water bottle could end up as a very soggy waterbed! An extremely good breeder would have introduced your puppy to the crate by letting two pups sleep together for a couple of nights, followed by several nights alone. How thankful you will be if you found that breeder.

Safe toys in the pup's crate or area will keep him occupied, but monitor their condition closely. Discard any toys that show signs of being chewed to bits. Squeaky parts, bits of stuffing or plastic or any other small pieces can cause intestinal blockage or possibly choking if ingested.

PROGRESSING WITH POTTY-TRAINING
After you've taken your puppy out and he has relieved himself in the area you've selected, he can have some free time with the

family as long as there is someone responsible for watching him. That doesn't mean just someone in the same room who is watching TV or busy on the computer, but one person who is doing nothing other than keeping an eye on the pup, playing with him on the floor and helping him understand his position in the pack.

This first taste of freedom will let you begin to set the house rules. If you don't want the dog on the furniture, now is the time to prevent his first attempts to jump up onto the couch. The word to use in this case is "Off," not "Down." "Down" is the word you will use to teach the down position, which is something entirely different.

Most corrections at this stage come in the form of simply distracting the puppy. Instead of telling him "No" for "Don't chew the carpet," distract the chomping puppy with a toy, and he'll forget about the carpet.

As you are playing with the pup, do not forget to watch him closely and pay attention to his body language. Whenever you see him begin to circle or sniff, take the puppy outside to relieve himself. If you are paper-training, put him back into his confined area on the newspapers. In either case, praise him as he eliminates while he actually is in the act of relieving himself. Three seconds after he has finished is too late!

You'll be praising him for running toward you, picking up a toy or whatever he may be doing at that moment, and that's not what you want to be praising him for. Timing is a vital tool in all dog training. Use it.

Remove soiled newspapers immediately and replace them with clean ones. You may want to take a small piece of soiled paper and place it in the middle of the new clean papers, as the scent will attract him to that spot when it's time to go again. That scent attraction is why it's so important to clean up any messes made in the house by using a product specially made to eliminate the odor of dog urine and droppings. Regular household cleansers won't do the trick. Pet shops sell the best pet deodorizers. Invest in the largest container you can find.

Scent attraction eventually will lead your pup to his chosen spot outdoors; this is the basis of outdoor training. When you take your puppy outside to relieve himself, use a one-word command such as "Outside" or "Go-potty" (that's one word to the puppy!) as you attach his leash. Then lead him to his area. Now comes the hard part—hard for you, that is. Just stand there until he urinates and defecates. Move him a few feet in one direction or another if he's just sitting there looking at you, but remember that this is neither playtime nor time for a

walk. This is strictly a business trip! Then, as he circles and squats (remember your timing!), give him a quiet "Good dog" as praise. If you start to jump for joy, ecstatic over his performance,

DAILY SCHEDULE

How many relief trips does your puppy need per day? A puppy up to the age of 14 weeks will need to go outside about 8 to 12 times per day. You will have to take the pup out any time he starts sniffing around the floor or turning in small circles, as well as after naps, meals, games and lessons or whenever he's released from his crate. Once the puppy is 14 to 22 weeks of age, he will require only 6 to 8 relief trips. At the ages of 22 to 32 weeks, the puppy will require about 5 to 7 trips. Adult dogs typically require 4 relief trips per day, in the morning, afternoon, evening and late at night.

he'll do one of two things: either he will stop mid-stream, as it were, or he'll do it again for you—in the house—and expect you to be just as delighted!

Give him five minutes or so and, if he doesn't go in that time, take him back indoors to his confined area and try again in another ten minutes, or immediately if you see him sniffing and circling. By careful observation, you'll soon work out a successful schedule.

Accidents, by the way, are just that—accidents. Clean them up quickly and thoroughly, without comment, after the puppy has been taken outside to finish his business and then put back into his area or crate. If you witness an accident in progress, say "No!" in a stern voice and get the pup

outdoors immediately. No punishment is needed. You and your puppy are just learning each other's language, and sometimes it's easy to miss a puppy's message. Chalk it up to experience and watch more closely from now on.

KEEPING THE PACK ORDERLY

Discipline is a form of training that brings order to life. For example, military discipline is what allows the soldiers in an army to work as one. Discipline is a form of teaching and, in dogs, is the basis of how the successful pack operates. Each member knows his place in the pack and all respect the leader, or alpha dog. It is essential for your puppy that you establish this type of relationship, with you as the alpha, or leader. It is a form of social coexistence that all canines recognize and accept. Discipline, therefore, is never to be confused with punishment. When you teach your puppy how you want him to behave, and he behaves properly and you praise him for it, you are disciplining him with a form of positive reinforcement.

For a dog, rewards come in the form of praise, a smile, a cheerful tone of voice, a few friendly pats or a rub of the ears. Rewards are also small food treats. Obviously, that does not mean bits of regular dog food. Instead, treats are very small bits

BASIC PRINCIPLES OF DOG TRAINING

1. Start training early. A young puppy is ready, willing and able.
2. Timing is your all-important tool. Praise at the exact time that the dog responds correctly. Pay close attention.
3. Patience is almost as important as timing!
4. Repeat! The same word has to mean the same thing every time.
5. In the beginning, praise all correct behavior verbally, along with treats and petting.

of special things like cheese or pieces of soft dog treats. The idea is to reward the dog with something very small that he can taste and swallow, providing instant positive reinforcement. If he has to take time to chew the treat, by the time he is finished he will have forgotten what he did to earn it!

Your puppy should never be physically punished. The displeasure shown on your face and in your voice is sufficient to signal to the pup that he has done something wrong. He wants to please everyone higher up on the social ladder, especially his leader, so a scowl and harsh voice will take care of the error. Growling out the word "Shame!" when the pup is caught in the act of doing something wrong is better than the repetitive "No." Some dogs hear "No" so often that they begin to think it's their name. By the way, do not use the dog's name when you're correcting him. His name is reserved to get his attention for something pleasant about to take place.

There are punishments that have nothing to do with you. For example, your dog may think that chasing cats is one reason for his existence. You can try to stop it as much as you like but without success because it's such fun for the dog. But one good hissing, spitting swipe of a cat's claws across the dog's nose will put an

KEEP IT SIMPLE—AND FUN

Keep your lessons simple, interesting and user-friendly. Fun breaks help you both. Spend two minutes or ten teaching your puppy, but practice only as long as your dog enjoys what he's doing and is focused on pleasing you. If he's bored or distracted, stop the training session after any correct response (always end on a high note!). After a few minutes of playtime, you can go back to "hitting the books."

end to the game forever. Intervene only when your dog's eyeball is seriously at risk. Cat scratches can cause permanent damage to an innocent but annoying puppy.

PUPPY KINDERGARTEN

COLLAR AND LEASH

Before you begin your Briard puppy's education, he must be used to his collar and leash. Choose a collar for your puppy that is secure, but not heavy or bulky. He won't enjoy training if he's uncomfortable. A flat buckle collar is fine for everyday wear and for initial puppy training. For older dogs, there are several types of training collars such as the martingale, which is a double loop that tightens slightly around the neck, or the head collar, which is similar to a horse's halter. Do not use any type of training collar unless you have been specifically shown how to put it on and how to use it. Ask your breeder or a recommended trainer for suggestions on what types of training collar are suitable for your Briard.

A lightweight 6-foot woven cotton or nylon training leash is preferred by most trainers because it is easy to fold up in your hand and comfortable to hold because there is a certain amount of give to it. There are lessons where the dog will start off 6 feet away from you at the end of the leash. The leash used to take the puppy outside to relieve himself is shorter because you don't want him to roam away from his area. The shorter leash will also be the one to use when you walk the puppy.

If you've been wise enough to enroll in a puppy kindergarten training class, suggestions will be made as to the best collar and leash for your young puppy. I say "wise" because your puppy will be in a class with puppies in his age range (up to five months old) of all breeds and sizes. It's the perfect way for him to learn the right way (and the wrong way) to interact with other dogs as well as their

LEASH TRAINING

House-training and leash training go hand in hand, literally. When taking your puppy outside to do his business, lead him there on his leash. Unless an emergency potty run is called for, do not whisk the puppy up into your arms and take him outside. If you have a fenced yard, you have the advantage of letting the puppy loose to go out, but it's better to put the dog on the leash and take him to his designated place in the yard until he is reliably house-trained. Taking the puppy for a walk is the best way to house-train a dog. The dog will associate the walk with his time to relieve himself, and the exercise of walking stimulates the dog's bowels and bladder. Dogs that are not trained to relieve themselves on a walk may hold it until they get back home, which of course defeats half the purpose of the walk.

Although herding is instinctual in the breed, not every Briard is equally good at the job. Some require more (and different) training.

people. You cannot teach your puppy how to interpret another dog's sign language. For a first-time puppy owner, these social-ization classes are invaluable. For experienced dog owners, they are a real boon to further training.

ATTENTION
You've been using the dog's name since the minute you collected him from the breeder, so you should be able to get his attention by saying his name—with a big smile and in an excited tone of voice. His response will be the puppy equivalent of "Here I am! What are we going to do?" Your immediate response (if you haven't guessed by now) is "Good dog." Rewarding him at the moment he pays attention to you teaches him the proper way to respond when he hears his name.

EXERCISES FOR A BASIC CANINE EDUCATION

THE SIT EXERCISE
There are several ways to teach the puppy to sit. The first one is to catch him whenever he is about to sit and, as his backside nears the floor, say "Sit, good dog!" That's positive reinforcement and, if your timing is sharp, he will learn that what he's doing at that second is connected to your saying "Sit" and that you think he's clever for doing it!

Another method is to start with the puppy on his leash in front of you. Show him a treat in the palm of your right hand. Bring your hand up under his nose and, almost in slow motion, move your hand up and back so his nose goes up in the air and his head tilts back as he follows the treat in your hand. At that point, he will

Most trainers begin with the sit command because it is generally the easiest for dogs to learn. Once success is met with the first command, the subsequent commands become easier.

two things at the same time. Both the verbal command and the motion of the hand are signals for the sit. Your puppy is watching you almost more than he is listening to you, so what you do is just as important as what you say.

Don't save any of these drills only for training sessions. Use them as much as possible at odd times during a normal day. The dog should always sit before being given his food dish. He should sit to let you go through a doorway first, when the doorbell rings or when you stop to speak to someone on the street.

have to either sit or fall over, so as his back legs buckle under, say "Sit, good dog," and then give him the treat and lots of praise. You may have to begin with your hand lightly running up his chest, actually lifting his chin up until he sits. Some (usually older) dogs require gentle pressure on their hindquarters with the left hand, in which case the dog should be on your left side. Puppies generally do not appreciate this physical dominance.

After a few times, you should be able to show the dog a treat in the open palm of your hand, raise your hand waist-high as you say "Sit" and have him sit. As a result, you will have taught him

TIPS FOR TRAINING AND SAFETY

1. Whether on or off leash, practice only in a fenced area.
2. Remove the training collar when the training session is over.
3. Don't try to break up a dog-fight.
4. "Come," "Leave it" and "Wait" are safety commands.
5. The dog belongs in a crate or behind a barrier when riding in the car.
6. Don't ignore the dog's first sign of aggression. Aggression only gets worse, so take it seriously.
7. Keep the faces of children and dogs separated.
8. Pay attention to what the dog is chewing.
9. Keep the vet's number near your phone.
10. "Okay" is a useful release command.

DOWN

"Down" is a harsh-sounding word and a submissive posture in dog body language, thus presenting two obstacles in teaching the down command. When the dog is about to flop down on his own, tell him "Good down." Pups that are not good about being handled learn better by having food lowered in front of them. A dog that trusts you can be gently guided into position. When you give the command "Down," be sure to say it sweetly!

THE DOWN EXERCISE

Before beginning to teach the down command, you must consider how the dog feels about this exercise. To him, "down" is a submissive position. Being flat on the floor with you standing over him is not his idea of fun. It's up to you to let him know that, while it may not be fun, the reward of your approval is worth his effort.

Start with the puppy on your left side in a sit position. Hold the leash right above his collar in your left hand. Have an extra-special treat, such as a small piece of cooked chicken or hot dog, in your right hand. Place it at the end of the pup's nose and steadily move your hand down and forward along the ground. Hold the leash to prevent a sudden lunge for the food. As the puppy goes into the down position, say

"Down" very gently.

The difficulty with this exercise is twofold: it's both the submissive aspect and the fact that most people say the word "Down" as if they were drill sergeants in charge of recruits! So issue the command sweetly, give him the treat and have the pup maintain the down position for several seconds. If he tries to get up immediately, place your hands on his shoulders and press down gently, giving him a very quiet "Good dog." As you progress with this lesson, increase the "down time" until he will hold it until you say "Okay" (his cue for release). Practice this one in the house at various times throughout the day.

By increasing the length of time during which the dog must maintain the down position, you'll find many uses for it. For example, he can lie at your feet in

Never use a forceful method to teach the down command. Once the Briard realizes that he is not being threatened in the down position, he will assume it without too much fuss.

the vet's office or anywhere that both of you have to wait, when you are on the phone, while the family is eating and so forth. If you progress to training for competitive obedience, he'll already be all set for the exercise called the "long down."

THE STAY EXERCISE

You can teach your Briard to stay in the sit, down and stand positions. To teach the sit/stay, have the dog sit on your left side. Hold the leash at waist level in your left hand and let the dog know that you have a treat in your closed right hand. Step forward on your right foot as you say "Stay." Immediately turn and stand directly in front of the dog, keeping your right hand up high so he'll keep his eye on the treat hand and maintain the sit position for a count of five. Return to your original position and offer the reward.

Increase the length of the sit/stay each time until the dog can hold it for at least 30 seconds without moving. After about a week of success, move out on your right foot and take two steps before turning to face the dog. Give the "Stay" hand signal (left palm back toward the dog's head) as you leave. He gets the treat when you return and he holds the sit/stay. Increase the distance that you walk away from him before turning until you reach the length

Practice the stay command in both the sit and down position. In time you can build up time and distance between you and the Briard.

of your training leash. But don't rush it! Go back to the beginning if he moves before he should. No matter what the lesson, never be upset by having to back up for a

command is not mastered at the easier levels. Above all, even if you do get frustrated, never let your puppy know! Always keep a positive, upbeat attitude during training, which will transmit to your dog for positive results.

The down/stay is taught in the same way once the dog is completely reliable and steady with the down command. Again, don't rush it. With the dog in the down position on your left side, step out on your right foot as you say "Stay." Return by walking around in back of the dog and into your original position. While you are training, it's okay to murmur something like "Hold on" to encourage him to stay put. When the dog will stay without moving when you are at a distance of 3 or 4 feet, begin to increase the length of time before you return. Be sure he holds the down on your return until you say "Okay." At that point, he gets his treat—just so he'll remember for next time that it's not over until it's over.

few days. The repetition and practice are what will make your dog reliable in these commands. It won't do any good to move on to something more difficult if the

THE COME EXERCISE

No command is more important to the safety of your Briard than "Come." It is what you should say every single time you see the puppy running toward you: "Jacques, come! Good dog." During playtime, run a few feet away from the puppy and turn and tell him to "Come" as he is already running to you. You can go so far as to teach

Training the Briard to heel at the owner's side is essential for a dog as powerful as this. Begin training the puppy to heel, and practice with the dog through-out his life.

Training the Briard to heel at the owner's side is essential for a dog as powerful as this. Begin training the puppy to heel, and practice with the dog throughout his life.

your puppy two things at once if you squat down and hold out your arms. As the pup gets close to you and you're saying "Good dog," bring your right arm in about waist high. Now he's also learning the hand signal, an excellent device should you be on the phone when you need to get him to come to you! You'll also both be one step ahead when you enter obedience classes.

When the puppy responds to your well-timed "Come," try it with the puppy on the training leash. This time, catch him off guard, while he's sniffing a leaf or watching a bird: "Jacques, come!" You may have to pause for a split second after his name to be sure you have his attention. If the puppy shows any sign of confusion, give the leash a mild

jerk and take a couple of steps backward. Do not repeat the command. In this case, you should say "Good come" as he reaches you.

That's the number-one rule of training. Each command word is given just once. Anything more is nagging. You'll also notice that all commands are one word only. Even when they are actually two words, you say them as one.

Never call the dog to come to you—with or without his name—if you are angry or intend to correct him for some misbehavior. When correcting the pup, you go to him. Your dog must always connect "Come" with something pleasant and with your approval; then you can rely on his response.

Puppies, like children, have notoriously short attention spans, so don't overdo it with any of the training. Keep each lesson short. Break it up with a quick run

COME AND GET IT!
The come command is your dog's safety signal. Until he is 99% perfect in responding, don't use the come command if you cannot enforce it. Practice on leash with treats or squeakers, or whenever the dog is running to you. Never call him to come to you if he is to be corrected for a misdemeanor. Reward the dog with a treat and happy praise whenever he comes to you.

around the yard or a ball toss, repeat the lesson and quit as soon as the pup gets it right. That way, you will always end with a "Good dog."

Life isn't perfect and neither are puppies. A time will come, often around ten months of age, when he'll become "selectively deaf" or choose to "forget" his name. He may respond by wagging his tail (and even seeming to smile at you) with a look that says "Make me!" Laugh, throw his favorite toy and skip the lesson you had planned. Pups will be pups!

THE HEEL EXERCISE

The second most important command to teach, after the come, is the heel. When you are walking your growing puppy, you need to be in control. Besides, it looks terrible to be pulled and yanked down the street, and it's not much fun either. Your eight- to ten-week-old puppy will probably follow you everywhere, but that's his natural instinct, not your control over the situation. However, any time he does follow you, you can say "Heel" and be ahead of the game, as he will learn to associate this command with the action of following you before you even begin teaching him to heel.

There is a very precise, almost military, procedure for teaching your dog to heel. As with all other obedience training, begin with the dog on your left side. He will be in

a very nice sit, and you will have the training leash across your chest. Hold the loop and folded leash in your right hand. Pick up the slack leash above the dog in your left hand and hold it loosely at your side. Step out on your left foot as you say "Heel." If the

RIGHT CLICK ON YOUR DOG

With three clicks, the dolphin jumps through the hoop. Wouldn't it be nice to have a dog who could obey wordless commands that easily? Clicker training actually was developed by dolphin trainers and today is used on dogs with great success. You can buy a clicker at a pet shop or pet-supply outlet, and then you'll be off and clicking.

You can click your dog into learning new commands, shaping or conditioning his behavior and solving bad habits. The clicker, used in conjunction with a treat, is an extension of positive reinforcement. The dog begins to recognize your happy clicking, and you will never have to rely on any other method. The dog is conditioned to follow your hand with the clicker, just as he would follow your hand with a treat. To discourage the dog from inappropriate behavior (like jumping up or barking), you can use the clicker to set a time frame and then click and reward the dog once he's waited the allotted time without jumping up or barking.

The cure for excessive pulling (a common problem) is to stop when the dog is no more than 2 or 3 feet ahead of you. Guide him back into position and begin again. With a really determined puller, try switching to a head collar. This will automatically turn the pup's head toward you so you can bring him back easily to the heel position. Give quiet, reassuring praise every time the leash goes slack and he's staying with you.

Staying and heeling can take a lot out of a dog, so provide playtime and free-running exercise to shake off the stress when the lessons are over. You don't want him to associate training with all work and no fun.

puppy does not move, give a gentle tug or pat your left leg to get him started. If he surges ahead of you, stop and pull him back gently until he is at your side. Tell him to sit and begin again.

Walk a few steps and stop while the puppy is correctly beside you. Tell him to sit and give mild verbal praise. (More enthusiastic praise will encourage him to think the lesson is over.) Repeat the lesson, increasing the number of steps you take only as long as the dog is heeling nicely beside you. When you end the lesson, have him hold the sit, then give him the "Okay" to let him know that this is the end of the lesson. Praise him so that he knows he did a good job.

TAPERING OFF TIDBITS

Your dog has been watching you—and the hand that treats—throughout all of his lessons, and now it's time to break the treat habit. Begin by giving him treats at the end of each lesson only. Then start to give a treat after the end of only some of the lessons. At the end of every lesson, as well as during the lessons, be consistent with the praise. Your pup now doesn't know whether he'll get a treat or not, but he should keep performing well just in case! Finally, you will stop giving treat rewards entirely. Save them for something brand-new that you want to teach him. Keep up the praise and you'll always have a "good dog."

OBEDIENCE CLASSES

The advantages of an obedience class are that your dog will have to learn amid the distractions of other people and dogs and that your mistakes will be quickly corrected by the trainer. Teaching your dog along with a qualified instructor and other handlers who may have more dog experience than you is another plus of the class environment. The instructor and other handlers can help you to find the most efficient way of teaching your dog a command or exercise. It's often easier to learn from other people's mistakes than your own. You will also learn all of the requirements for competitive obedience trials, in which you can earn titles and go on to advanced jumping and retrieving exercises, which are fun for many dogs. Obedience classes build the foundation needed for many other canine activities.

NO MORE TREATS

When your dog is responding promptly and correctly to commands, it's time to eliminate treats. Begin by alternating a treat reward with a verbal-praise-only reward. Gradually eliminate all treats while increasing the frequency of praise. Overlook pleading eyes and expectant expressions, but if he's still watching your treat hand, you're on your way to using hand signals.

TRAINING FOR OTHER ACTIVITIES

Once your dog has basic obedience under his collar and is 12 months of age, you can enter the world of agility training. Dogs think agility is pure fun, like being turned loose in an amusement park full of obstacles! In addition to agility, there are hunting activities for sporting dogs, lure-coursing events for sighthounds, go-to-ground events for terriers, racing for the Nordic sled dogs, herding trials for the shepherd breeds and tracking, which is open to all "nosey" dogs (which would include all dogs!). For those who like to volunteer, there is the wonderful feeling of owning a therapy dog and visiting hospices, nursing homes and veterans' homes to bring smiles, comfort and companionship to those who live there.

Around the house, your Briard can be taught to do some simple chores. You might teach him to carry some small household items or to fetch the morning newspaper. The kids can teach the dog all kinds of tricks, from playing hide-and-seek to balancing a biscuit on his nose. A family dog is what rounds out the family. Everything he does, including sitting at your feet and gazing lovingly at you, represents the bonus of owning a dog.

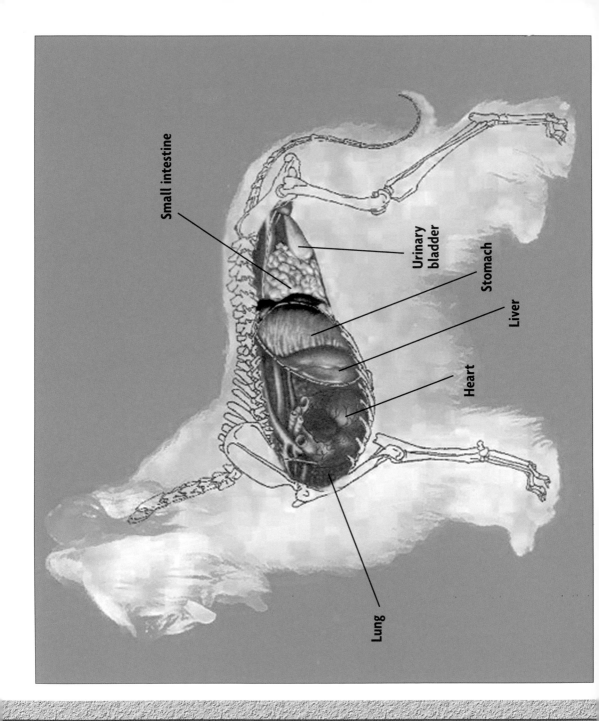

Small intestine

Urinary bladder

Stomach

Liver

Heart

Lung

INTERNAL ORGANS OF THE BRIARD

BRIARD

By Lowell Ackerman DVM, DACVD

HEALTHCARE FOR A LIFETIME

When you own a dog, you become his healthcare advocate over his entire lifespan, as well as being the one to shoulder the financial burden of such care. Accordingly, it is worthwhile to focus on prevention rather than treatment, as you and your pet will both be happier.

Of course, the best place to have begun your program of preventive healthcare is with the initial purchase or adoption of your dog. There is no way of guaranteeing that your new furry friend is free of medical problems, but there are some things you can do to improve the odds. You certainly should have done adequate research into the Briard and have selected your puppy carefully rather than buying on impulse. Health issues aside, a large number of pet abandonment and relinquishment cases arise from a mismatch between pet needs and owner expectations. This is entirely preventable with appropriate planning and finding a good breeder.

Regarding healthcare issues specifically, it is very difficult to make blanket statements about where to acquire a problem-free pet, but, again, a reputable breeder is your best bet. In an ideal situation you have the opportunity to see both parents, get references from other owners of the breeder's pups and see genetic-testing documentation for several generations of the litter's ancestors. At the very least, you must thoroughly investigate the Briard and the problems inherent in that breed, as well as the genetic testing available to screen for those problems. Genetic testing offers some important benefits but is available for only a few disorders in a relatively small number of breeds and is not available for some of the most common genetic diseases, such as hip dysplasia, cataracts, epilepsy, cardiomyopathy, etc. This area of research is indeed exciting and increasingly important, and advances will continue to be made each year. In fact, recent research has shown that there is an equivalent dog gene for 75% of known human genes, so research done in either species is likely to benefit the other.

We've also discussed that evaluating the behavioral nature of your Briard and that of his immediate family members is an important part of the selection process that cannot be overemphasized. It is sometimes difficult to evaluate temperament in puppies because certain behavioral tendencies, such as some forms of aggression, may not be immediately evident. More dogs are euthanized each year for behavioral reasons than for all medical conditions combined, so it is critical to take temperament issues seriously. Start with a well-balanced, friendly companion and put the time and effort into proper socialization, and you will be

rewarded with a valued relationship for the life of the dog.

Assuming that you have started off with a pup from healthy, sound stock, you then become responsible for helping your veterinarian keep your pet healthy. Some crucial things happen before you even bring your puppy home. Parasite control typically begins at two weeks of age, and vaccinations typically begin at six to eight weeks of age. A pre-pubertal evaluation is typically scheduled for about six months of age. At this time, a dental evaluation is done (since the adult teeth are now in), heartworm prevention is started and neutering or spaying is most commonly done.

It is critical to commence regular dental care at home if you have not already done so. It may not sound very important, but most dogs have active periodontal disease by four years of age if they don't have their teeth cleaned regularly at home, not just at their veterinary exams. Dental problems lead to more than just bad "doggy breath." Gum disease can have very serious medical consequences. If you start brushing your dog's teeth and using antiseptic rinses from a young age, your dog will be accustomed to it and will not resist. The results will be healthy dentition, which your pet will need to enjoy a long, healthy life.

Many dogs are considered adults at a year of age, but the Briard reaches adulthood when he

It is vital to take proper care of your Briard's teeth, as dental problems can lead to other more serious health conditions.

is around 18 months old. Even individual dogs within each breed have different healthcare requirements, so work with your veterinarian to determine what will be needed and what your role should be. This doctor-client relationship is important because as vaccination guidelines change, there may not be an annual "vaccine visit" scheduled. You must make sure that you see your veterinarian at least annually, even if no vaccines are due, because this is the best opportunity to coordinate healthcare activities and to make sure

that no medical issues creep by unaddressed.

When your Briard reaches three-quarters of his anticipated lifespan, he is considered a "senior" and likely requires some special care. In general, if you've been taking great care of your canine companion throughout his formative and adult years, the transition to senior status should be a smooth one. Age is not a disease, and as long as everything is functioning as it should, there is no reason why most of late adulthood should not be rewarding for both

Don't Eat the Daisies!

Many plants and flowers are beautiful to look at, but can be highly toxic if ingested by your dog. Reactions range from abdominal pain and vomiting to convulsions and death. If the following plants are in your home, remove them. If they are outside your house or in your garden, avoid accidents by making sure your dog is never left unsupervised in those locations.

Azalea	Dumb cane	Mescal bean
Belladonna	Dutchman's breeches	Mushrooms
Bird of paradise	Elephant's ear	Nightshade
Bulbs	Hydrangea	Philodendron
Calla lily	Jack-in-the-pulpit	Poinsettia
Cardinal flower	Jasmine	*Prunus* species
Castor bean	Jimsonweed	Tobacco
Chinaberry tree	Larkspur	Yellow jasmine
Daphne	Laurel	Yews, *Taxus* species
	Lily of the valley	

you and your pet. This is especially true if you have tended to the details, such as regular veterinary visits, proper dental care, excellent nutrition and management of bone and joint issues.

At this stage in your Briard's life, your veterinarian may want to schedule visits twice yearly, instead of once, to run some laboratory screenings, electrocardiograms and the like, and to change the diet to something more digestible. Catching problems early is the best way to manage them effectively. Treating the early stages of heart disease is so much easier than trying to intervene when there is more significant damage to the heart muscle. Similarly, managing the beginning of kidney problems is fairly routine if there is no significant kidney damage. Other problems, like cognitive dysfunc-

tion (similar to senility and Alzheimer's disease), cancer, diabetes and arthritis, are more common in older dogs, but all can be treated to help the dog live as many happy, comfortable years as possible. Just as in people, medical management is more effective (and less expensive) when you catch things early.

SELECTING A VETERINARIAN
There is probably no more important decision that you will make regarding your pet's health-care than the selection of his doctor. Your pet's veterinarian will be a pediatrician, family-practice physician and gerontologist, depending on the dog's life stage, and will be the individual who makes recommendations regarding issues such as when specialists need to be consulted, when

ELEVATED BOWLS

Feeding your dog from elevated bowls has been long thought to be an effective bloat preventive, but new research suggests that may not be the case. Some owners feed their dogs from elevated bowls to prevent their eating too rapidly, but it is sometimes now advised not to feed from elevated bowls if dealing with a bloat-prone breed. Unfortunately, there is no surefire way to prevent bloat, and even the causes are not known for sure. Use common sense and know your dog so that you can recognize the signs when his health is compromised and get to the vet right away.

diagnostic testing and/or therapeutic intervention is needed and when you will need to seek outside emergency and critical-care services. Your vet will act as your advocate and liaison throughout these processes.

Everyone has his own idea about what to look for in a vet, an individual who will play a big role in his dog's (and, of course, his own) life for many years to come. For some, it is the compassionate caregiver with whom they hope to develop a professional relationship to span the lifetime of their dogs and even their future pets. For others, they are seeking a clinician with keen diagnostic and therapeutic insight who can deliver state-of-the-art healthcare. Still others need a veterinary facility that is open evenings and weekends, is in close proximity or provides mobile veterinary services to accommodate their schedules; these people may not much mind that their dogs might see different veterinarians on each visit. Just as we have different reasons for selecting our own healthcare professionals (e.g., covered by insurance plan, expert in field, convenient location, etc.), we should not expect that there is a one-size-fits-all recommendation for selecting a veterinarian and veterinary practice. The best advice is to be honest in your assessment of what you expect from a veterinary practice and to conscien-

tiously research the options in your area. You will quickly appreciate that not all veterinary practices are the same, and you will be happiest with one that truly meets your needs.

There is another point to be considered in the selection of veterinary services. Not that long ago, a single veterinarian would attempt to manage all medical and surgical issues as they arose. That was often problematic because veterinarians are trained in many species and many diseases, and it was just impossible for general veterinary practitioners to be experts in every species, every breed, every field and every ailment. However, just as in the human healthcare fields, special-ization has allowed general practi-tioners to concentrate on primary healthcare delivery, especially wellness and the prevention of infectious diseases, and to utilize a network of specialists to assist in the management of conditions that require specific expertise and experience. Thus there are now many types of veterinary special-ists, including dermatologists, cardiologists, ophthalmologists, surgeons, internists, oncologists, neurologists, behaviorists, critical-ists and others to help primary-care veterinarians deal with compli-cated medical challenges. In most cases, specialists see cases referred by primary-care veterinarians, make diagnoses and set up management plans. From there, the animals' ongoing care is returned to their primary-care veterinarians. This important team approach to your pet's medical-care needs has provided opportunities for advanced care and an unparalleled level of quality to be delivered.

With all of the opportunities for your Briard to receive high-quality veterinary medical care, there is another topic that needs to be addressed at the same time—cost. It's been said that you can have excellent healthcare or inexpensive healthcare, but never both; this is as true in veterinary medicine as it is in human medicine. While veterinary costs are a fraction of what the same services cost in the human health-care arena, it is still difficult to deal with unanticipated medical costs, especially since they can easily creep into hundreds or even thousands of dollars if specialists or emergency services become involved. However, there are ways of managing these risks. The easiest is to buy pet health insurance and realize that its foremost purpose is not to cover routine healthcare visits but rather to serve as an umbrella for those rainy days when your pet needs medical care and you don't want to worry about whether or not you can afford that care.

Pet insurance policies are very cost-effective (and very inexpen-

SAMPLE VACCINATION SCHEDULE

6–8 weeks of age	Parvovirus, Distemper, Adenovirus-2 (Hepatitis)
9–11 weeks of age	Parvovirus, Distemper, Adenovirus-2 (Hepatitis)
12–14 weeks of age	Parvovirus, Distemper, Adenovirus-2 (Hepatitis)
16–20 weeks of age	Rabies
1 year of age	Parvovirus, Distemper, Adenovirus-2 (Hepatitis), Rabies

Revaccination is performed every one to three years, depending on the product, the method of administration and the patient's risk. Initial adult inoculation (for dogs at least 16 weeks of age in which a puppy series was not done or could not be confirmed) is two vaccinations, done three to four weeks apart, with revaccination according to the same criteria mentioned. Other vaccines are given as decided between owner and veterinarian.

sive by human health-insurance standards), but make sure that you buy the policy long before you intend to use it (preferably starting in puppyhood because coverage will exclude pre-existing conditions) and that you are actually buying an indemnity insurance plan from an insurance company that is regulated by your state or province. Many insurance policy look-alikes are actually discount clubs that are redeemable only at specific locations and for specific services. An indemnity plan covers your pet at almost all veterinary, specialty and emergency practices and is an excellent way to manage your pet's ongoing healthcare needs.

VACCINATIONS AND INFECTIOUS DISEASES

There has never been an easier time to prevent a variety of infectious diseases in your dog, but the advances we've made in veterinary medicine come with a price— choice. Now while it may seem that choice is a good thing (and it is), it has never been more difficult for the pet owner (or the veterinarian) to make an informed decision about the best way to protect pets through vaccination.

Years ago, it was just accepted that puppies got a starter series of vaccinations and then annual "boosters" throughout their lives to keep them protected. As more and more vaccines became available,

consumers wanted the convenience of having all of that protection in a single injection. The result was "multivalent" vaccines that crammed a lot of protection into a single syringe. The manufacturers' recommendations were to give the vaccines annually, and this was a simple enough protocol to follow. However, as veterinary medicine has become more sophisticated and we have started looking more at healthcare quandaries rather than convenience, it became necessary to reevaluate the situation and deal with some tough questions. It is important to realize that whether or not to use a particular vaccine depends on the risk of contracting the disease against which it protects, the severity of the disease if it is contracted, the duration of immunity provided by the vaccine, the safety of the product and the needs of the individual animal. In a very general sense, rabies, distemper, hepatitis and parvovirus are considered core vaccine needs, while parainfluenza, *Bordetella bronchiseptica*, leptospirosis, coronavirus and borreliosis (Lyme disease) are considered non-core needs and best reserved for animals that demonstrate reasonable risk of contracting the diseases.

NEUTERING/SPAYING

Sterilization procedures (neutering for males/spaying for females) are

COMMON INFECTIOUS DISEASES

Let's discuss some of the diseases that create the need for vaccination in the first place. Following are the major canine infectious diseases and a simple explanation of each.

Rabies: A devastating viral disease that can be fatal in dogs and people. In fact, vaccination of dogs and cats is an important public-health measure to create a resistant animal buffer population to protect people from contracting the disease. Vaccination schedules are determined on a government level and are not optional for pet owners; rabies vaccination is required by law in all 50 states.

Parvovirus: A severe, potentially life-threatening disease that is easily transmitted between dogs. There are four strains of the virus, but it is believed that there is significant "cross-protection" between strains that may be included in individual vaccines.

Distemper: A potentially severe and life-threatening disease with a relatively high risk of exposure, especially in certain regions. In very high-risk distemper environments, young pups may be vaccinated with human measles vaccine, a related virus that offers cross-protection when administered at four to ten weeks of age.

Hepatitis: Caused by canine adenovirus type 1 (CAV-1), but since vaccination with the causative virus has a higher rate of adverse effects, cross-protection is derived from the use of adenovirus type 2 (CAV-2), a cause of respiratory disease and one of the potential causes of canine cough. Vaccination with CAV-2 provides long-term immunity against hepatitis, but relatively less protection against respiratory infection.

Canine cough: Also called tracheobronchitis, actually a fairly complicated result of viral and bacterial offenders; therefore, even with vaccination, protection is incomplete. Wherever dogs congregate, canine cough will likely be spread among them. Intranasal vaccination with *Bordetella* and parainfluenza is the best safeguard, but the duration of immunity does not appear to be very long, typically a year at most. These are non-core vaccines, but vaccination is sometimes mandated by boarding kennels, obedience classes, dog shows and other places where dogs congregate to try to minimize spread of infection.

Leptospirosis: A potentially fatal disease that is more common in some geographic regions. It is capable of being spread to humans. The disease varies with the individual "serovar," or strain, of *Leptospira* involved. Since there does not appear to be much cross-protection between serovars, protection is only as good as the likelihood that the serovar in the vaccine is the same as the one in the pet's local environment. Problems with *Leptospira* vaccines are that protection does not last very long, side effects are not uncommon and a large percentage of dogs (perhaps 30%) may not respond to vaccination.

Borrelia burgdorferi: The cause of Lyme disease, the risk of which varies with the geographic area in which the pet lives and travels. Lyme disease is spread by deer ticks in the eastern US and western black-legged ticks in the western part of the country, and the risk of exposure is high in some regions. Lameness, fever and inappetence are most commonly seen in affected dogs. The extent of protection from the vaccine has not been conclusively demonstrated.

Coronavirus: This disease has a high risk of exposure, especially in areas where dogs congregate, but it typically causes only mild to moderate digestive upset (diarrhea, vomiting, etc.). Vaccines are available, but the duration of protection is believed to be relatively short and the effectiveness of the vaccine in preventing infection is considered low.

There are many other vaccinations available, including those for *Giardia* and canine adenovirus-1. While there may be some specific indications for their use, and local risk factors to be considered, they are not widely recommended for most dogs.

meant to accomplish several purposes. While the underlying premise is to address the risk of pet overpopulation, there are also some medical and behavioral benefits to the surgeries as well. For females, spaying prior to the first estrus (heat cycle) leads to a marked reduction in the risk of mammary cancer and other serious female health problems. There also will be no manifestations of "heat" to attract male dogs and no bleeding in the house. For males, there is prevention of testicular cancer and a reduction in the risk of prostate problems. In both sexes there may be some limited reduction in aggressive behaviors toward other dogs, and some diminishing of urine marking, roaming and mounting.

While neutering and spaying do indeed prevent animals from contributing to pet overpopulation, even no-cost and low-cost neutering options have not eliminated the problem. Perhaps one of the main reasons for this is that individuals that intentionally breed their dogs and those that allow their animals to run at large are the main causes of unwanted offspring. Also, animals in shelters are often there because they were abandoned or relinquished, not because they came from unplanned matings. Neutering/spaying is important, but it should be considered in the context of the real causes of animals' ending up in shelters and eventually being euthanized.

One of the important considerations regarding neutering is that it is a surgical procedure. This sometimes gets lost in discussions of low-cost procedures and commoditization of the process. In females, spaying is specifically referred to as an ovariohysterectomy. In this procedure, a midline incision is made in the abdomen and the entire uterus and both ovaries are surgically removed. While this is a major invasive surgical procedure, it usually has few complications because it is typically performed on healthy young animals. However, it is major surgery, as any woman who has had a hysterectomy will attest.

In males, neutering has traditionally referred to castration, which involves the surgical removal of both testicles. While still a significant piece of surgery, there is not the abdominal exposure that is required in the female surgery. In addition, there is now a chemical sterilization option, in which a solution is injected into each testicle, leading to atrophy of the sperm-producing cells. This can typically be done under sedation rather than full anesthesia. This is a relatively new approach, and there are no long-term clinical studies yet available.

Neutering/spaying is typically

done around six months of age at most veterinary hospitals, although techniques have been pioneered to perform the procedures in animals as young as eight weeks of age. In general, the surgeries on the very young animals are done for the specific reason of sterilizing them before they go to their new homes. This is done in some shelter hospitals for assurance that the animals will definitely not produce any pups. Otherwise, these organizations need to rely on owners to comply with their wishes to have the animals "altered" at a later date, something that does not always happen.

There are some exciting immunocontraceptive "vaccines" currently under development, and there may be a time when contraception in pets will not require surgical procedures. We anxiously await these developments.

EYE PROBLEMS IN THE BRIARD

RETINAL PIGMENT EPITHELIAL DYSTROPHY (RPED)

Research is ongoing concerning retinal pigment epithelial dystrophy (RPED), a condition that causes reduced vision in the Briard. This condition is also referred to as central progressive retinal atrophy.

What a lot of great long words this condition presents. If we look at the anatomy of the eye, we can understand these words and the diseases they describe a little better. The pigment epithelium is the first part of the retina that the light falls on. Both humans and Briards see things when the light falls on the next layer down, the rods and cones, and the message that light is coming into the eye goes off to the brain through the nerve cells. The pigment cells support the rods and cones, both physically and by providing them with oxygen and food in the form of the sugar glucose.

Retinal pigment epithelial dystrophy means abnormality of the pigment cell layer of the retina. The retina is the light-sensitive "skin" or epithelium at the back of the eye. In RPED, the pigment cells do not work properly, and as a result the rods and cones die. As the light coming through the eye lands on dead rods and cones, the light energy cannot be transformed into electrical energy to go off to the brain, and so the dog cannot see anything in the area of the retina where the cells have died. In RPED, the rods and cones that die are the ones for vision immediately in front, leaving the dog with vision just around the edges.

RPED is a genetic illness that seems to be found more commonly in the Briards of Britain than the rest of the world. However, Professor Peter Bedford of the UK feels that there are other factors at work as well; he and his research team are conducting studies on this

DO YOU KNOW ABOUT HIP DYSPLASIA?

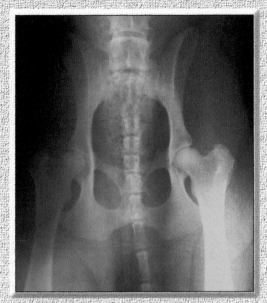

X-ray of a dog with "Good" hips.

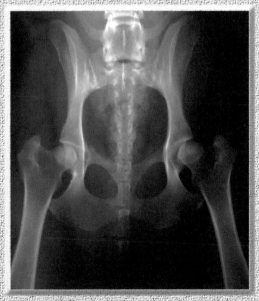

X-ray of a dog with "Moderate" dysplastic hips.

Hip dysplasia is a fairly common condition found in pure-bred dogs. When a dog has hip dysplasia, his hind leg has an incorrectly formed hip joint. By constant use of the hip joint, it becomes more and more loose, wears abnormally and may become arthritic.

Hip dysplasia can only be confirmed with an x-ray, but certain symptoms may indicate a problem. Your dog may have a hip dysplasia problem if he walks in a peculiar manner, hops instead of smoothly runs, uses his hind legs in unison (to keep the pressure off the weak joint), has trouble getting up from a prone position or always sits with both legs together on one side of his body.

As the dog matures, he may adapt well to life with a bad hip, but in a few years the arthritis develops and many dogs with hip dysplasia become crippled.

Hip dysplasia is considered an inherited disease and can be diagnosed definitively by x-ray only when the dog is two years old, although symptoms often appear earlier. Some experts claim that a special diet might help your puppy outgrow the bad hip, but the usual treatments are surgical. The removal of the pectineus muscle, the removal of the round part of the femur, reconstructing the pelvis and replacing the hip with an artificial one are all surgical interventions that are expensive, but they are usually very successful. Follow the advice of your veterinarian.

disease. He and his team have discovered that the disease is most likely to be the result of a liver deficiency, which means that essential chemicals derived from vitamin E are not transported to the retina. Without these chemicals, the pigment cells cannot work properly and die. The liver deficiency is the inherited part of the illness, and the only sign that a Briard has inherited RPED comes when parts of the retina start to die and the dog's vision is reduced.

The eye team also believes that the amount of liver deficiency inherited is variable, so the amount of retinal damage varies as well. The amount of vitamin E in the diet can also alter the amount of retinal damage the Briard suffers. If the dog is fed a diet rich in vitamin E, it can help the liver produce the chemical derivatives that the retina needs, reducing the severity of the retinal damage.

Eye-screening schemes have helped reduce the incidence of this illness. Regular eye checks have discovered the dogs with retinal damage because it is relatively easy to look at the retina directly with the correct opththalmoscope if you have had the correct training (and the dog has had the correct training to keep still!). Breeders have avoided using Briards with the liver deficiency factor in breeding programs, and with the advent of complete canine diets, dogs are being fed quality food that contains all the vitamins that are needed.

Professor Bedford is working on the liver defect to work out exactly what is going wrong, and he is hoping to be able to develop a DNA test so it will be possible to check if a dog is carrying the gene for RPED from a blood test long before there are any disturbances in vision.

STATIONARY NIGHT BLINDNESS

Stationary night blindness is inherited as a recessive illness. This means that the gene for normal sight covers the presence of the faulty gene: normal is dominant to stationary night blindness, and stationary night blindness is recessive to normal sight. Research on stationary night blindness is more advanced than that for RPED because the genetic mutation has been isolated, and there is a test to see if your Briard carries the faulty gene.

Before the genetic test was available, it was impossible to find out if a dog was a carrier until it became the parent of an affected puppy when it was mated to another carrier. Now a simple blood test can tell if your Briard is affected, is a carrier or is clear of the problem. The blood test is an easier examination than the electroretinogram, which is a recording of the eye's electrical response to a flash of light.

An affected Briard will have no vision at night from six weeks of age, but the amount of daylight vision is variable. Some affected dogs will have normal vision in daylight, while others may have mild visual loss and others severe loss of vision despite the daylight.

The reason that this is called stationary night blindness is that the extent of the visual damage is apparent from the age of six weeks, and it does not deteriorate. It was first described in humans in France, in 1831, when a 16-year-old conscript claimed exemption from military service because he could not see in the dark. Unfortunately he was not believed at first, but after a period of service he was re-examined and gained his exemption. His father, grandfather and great-grandfather all had this problem, which was traced back to a butcher, Jean Nougaret, who had been born in 1637. This is the longest known human pedigree of a genetic illness.

The problem with stationary night blindness is with the special cells that pick up light signals. There are two types of receptor cells in the retina of the eye: the rods and the cones. The cones are concerned with color vision and the rods with vision when there is little light. This is why we cannot see colors properly when it is dark.

In stationary night blindness, the problem is with the rods. When light falls on them, the pigment they contain, rhodopsin or visual purple, is bleached by the light. In a normal retina, it is soon returned to its original form, ready to be bleached by light again. Each time it is bleached, it sends a signal to the brain, telling it that light is present.

In those with stationary night blindness, this process goes wrong. The rod acts as though it is being constantly bombarded by light, making it no longer sensitive enough to pick up the dim light from things in the dark.

Rhodopsin is made from vitamin A, and vitamin A is derived from carotene as found in carrots. Those with vitamin-A deficiency also suffer from night blindness, so there is some truth in the saying that carrots help you see in the dark. Now that the blood test is easily available, it should be possible to eradicate the genetic form of stationary night blindness from the Briard.

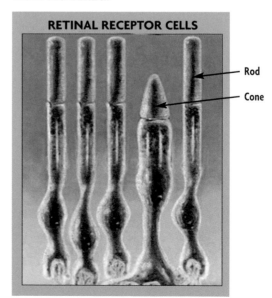

RETINAL RECEPTOR CELLS

Rod

Cone

A scanning electron micrograph of a dog flea, *Ctenocephalides canis,* on dog hair.

EXTERNAL PARASITES

FLEAS

Fleas have been around for millions of years and, while we have better tools now for controlling them than at any time in the past, there still is little chance that they will end up on an endangered species list. Actually, they are very well adapted to living on our pets, and they continue to adapt as we make advances.

The female flea can consume 15 times her weight in blood during active reproduction and can lay as many as 40 eggs a day. These eggs are very resistant to the effects of insecticides. They hatch into larvae, which then mature and spin cocoons. The immature fleas reside in this pupal stage until the time is right for feeding. This pupal stage is also very resistant to the effects of insecticides, and pupae can last in the environment without feeding for many months. Newly emergent fleas are attracted to animals by the warmth of the animals' bodies, movement and exhaled carbon dioxide. However, when they first emerge from their cocoons, they orient towards light; thus when an animal passes between a flea and the light source, casting a shadow, the flea pounces and starts to feed. If the animal turns out to be a dog or cat, the reproductive cycle continues. If the flea lands on another type of animal, including a person, the flea will bite but will then look for a more appropriate host. An emerging adult flea can survive without feeding for up to 12 months but, once it tastes blood, it can survive off its host for only 3 to 4 days.

It was once thought that fleas spend most of their lives in the environment, but we now know that fleas won't willingly jump off a dog unless leaping to another dog or when physically removed by brushing, bathing or other manipulation. Flea eggs, on the other hand, are shiny and smooth, and they roll off the animal and into the environment. The eggs, larvae and pupae then exist in the environment, but once the adult finds a susceptible animal, it's home sweet home until the flea is forced to seek refuge elsewhere.

Since adult fleas live on the animal and immature forms survive in the environment, a successful treatment plan must address all stages of the flea life cycle. There are now several safe and effective flea-control products that can be applied on a monthly

FLEA PREVENTION FOR YOUR DOG

- Discuss with your veterinarian the safest product to protect your dog, likely in the form of a monthly tablet or a liquid preparation placed on the back of the dog's neck.
- For dogs suffering from flea-bite dermatitis, a shampoo or topical insecticide treatment is required.
- Your lawn and property should be sprayed with an insecticide designed to kill fleas and ticks that lurk outdoors.
- Using a flea comb, check the dog's coat regularly for any signs of parasites.
- Practice good housekeeping. Vacuum floors, carpets and furniture regularly, especially in the areas that the dog frequents, and wash the dog's bedding weekly.
- Follow up house-cleaning with carpet shampoos and sprays to rid the house of fleas at all stages of development. Insect growth regulators are the safest option.

basis. These include fipronil, imidacloprid, selamectin and permethrin (found in several formulations). Most of these products have significant flea-killing rates within 24 hours. However, none of them will control the immature forms in the environment. To accomplish this, there are a variety of insect growth regulators that can be

THE FLEA'S LIFE CYCLE

What came first, the flea or the egg? This age-old mystery is more difficult to comprehend than the actual cycle of the flea. Fleas usually live only about four months. A female can lay 2,000 eggs in her lifetime.

Photo by Carolina Biological Supply Co.

Egg

After ten days of rolling around your carpet or under your furniture, the eggs hatch into larvae, which feed on various and sundry debris. In days or months, depending on the climate, the larvae spin cocoons and develop into the pupal or nymph stage, which quickly develop into fleas.

Larva

Photo by Carolina Biological Supply Co.

Pupa

These immature fleas must locate a host within 10 to 14 days or they will die. Only about 1% of the flea population exist as adult fleas, while the other 99% exist as eggs, larvae or pupae.

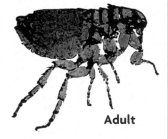

Adult

KILL FLEAS THE NATURAL WAY

If you choose not to go the route of conventional medication, there are some natural ways to ward off fleas:

• Dust your dog with a natural flea powder, composed of such herbal goodies as rosemary, wormwood, pennyroyal, citronella, rue, tobacco powder and eucalyptus.

• Apply diatomaceous earth, the fossilized remains of single-cell algae, to your carpets, furniture and pet's bedding. Even though it's not good for dogs, it's even worse for fleas, which will dry up swiftly and die.

• Brush your dog frequently, give him adequate exercise and let him fast occasionally. All of these activities strengthen the dog's immune system and make him more resistant to disease and parasites.

• Bathe your dog with a capful of pennyroyal or eucalyptus oil.

• Feed a natural diet, free of additives and preservatives. Add some fresh garlic and brewer's yeast to the dog's morning portion, as these items have flea-repelling properties.

sprayed into the environment (e.g., pyriproxyfen, methoprene, fenoxycarb) as well as insect development inhibitors such as lufenuron that can be administered. These compounds have no effect on adult fleas, but they stop immature forms from developing into adults. In years gone by, we relied heavily on toxic insecticides (such as organophosphates, organochlorines and carbamates) to manage the flea problem, but today's options are not only much safer to use on our pets but also safer for the environment.

TICKS

Ticks are members of the spider class (arachnids) and are blood-sucking parasites capable of transmitting a variety of diseases, including Lyme disease, ehrlichiosis, babesiosis and Rocky Mountain spotted fever. It's easy to see ticks on your own skin, but it is more of a challenge when your furry companion is affected. Whenever you happen to be planning a stroll in a tick-infested area (especially forests, grassy or wooded areas or parks) be prepared to do a thorough inspection of your dog afterward to search for ticks. Ticks can be tricky, so make sure you spend time looking in the ears, between the toes and everywhere else where a tick might hide. Ticks need to be attached for 24–72 hours before they transmit most of the diseases that they carry, so you do have a window of opportunity for some preventive intervention.

S. E. M. BY PHOTOTAKE.

A scanning electron micrograph of the head of a female deer tick, *Ixodes dammini*, a parasitic tick that carries Lyme disease.

A TICKING BOMB

There is nothing good about a tick's harpooning his nose into your dog's skin. Among the diseases caused by ticks are Rocky Mountain spotted fever, canine ehrlichiosis, canine babesiosis, canine hepatozoonosis and Lyme disease. If a dog is allergic to the saliva of a female wood tick, he can develop tick paralysis.

Female ticks live to eat and breed. They can lay between 4,000 and 5,000 eggs and they die soon after. Males, on the other hand, live only to mate with the females and continue the process as long as they are able. Most ticks live on multiple hosts before parasitizing dogs. The immature forms typically reside on grass and shrubs, waiting for susceptible animals to walk by. The larvae and nymph stages typically feed on wildlife.

If only a few ticks are present on a dog, they can be plucked out, but it is important to remove the entire head and mouthparts,

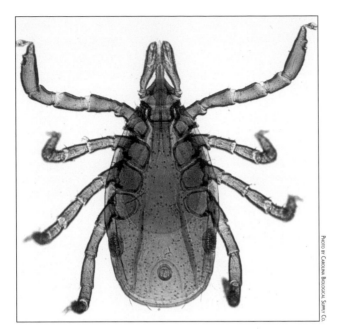

Photo by Carolina Biological Supply Co.

Deer tick,
Ixodes dammini.

which may be deeply embedded in the skin. This is best accomplished with forceps designed especially for this purpose; fingers can be used but should be protected with rubber gloves, plastic wrap or at least a paper towel. The tick should be grasped as closely as possible to the animal's skin and should be pulled upward with steady, even pressure. Do not squeeze, crush or puncture the body of the tick or you risk exposure to any disease carried by that tick. Once the ticks have been removed, the sites of attachment should be disinfected. Your hands should then be washed with soap and water to further minimize risk of contagion. The tick should be disposed of in a container of alcohol or household bleach.

Some of the newer flea products, specifically those with fipronil, selamectin and permethrin, have effect against some, but not all, species of tick. Flea collars containing appropriate pesticides (e.g., propoxur, chlorfen-vinphos) can aid in tick control. In most areas, such collars should be placed on animals in March, at the beginning of the tick season, and changed regularly. Leaving the collar on when the pesticide level is waning invites the development of resistance. Amitraz collars are also good for tick control, and the active ingredient does not interfere with other flea-control products. The ingredient helps prevent the attachment of ticks to the skin and will cause those ticks already on the skin to detach themselves.

TICK CONTROL

Removal of underbrush and leaf litter and the thinning of trees in areas where tick control is desired are recommended. These actions remove the cover and food sources for small animals that serve as hosts for ticks. With continued mowing of grasses in these areas, the probability of ticks' surviving is further reduced. A variety of insecticide ingredients (e.g., resmethrin, carbaryl, permethrin, chlorpyrifos, dioxathion and allethrin) are registered for tick control around the home.

MITES

Mites are tiny arachnid parasites that parasitize the skin of dogs. Skin diseases caused by mites are referred to as "mange," and there are many different forms seen in dogs. These forms are very different from one another, each one warranting an individual description.

Sarcoptic mange, or scabies, is one of the itchiest conditions that affects dogs. The microscopic *Sarcoptes* mites burrow into the superficial layers of the skin and can drive dogs crazy with itchiness. They are also communicable to people, although they can't complete their reproductive cycle on people. In addition to being tiny, the mites also are often difficult to find when trying to make a diagnosis. Skin scrapings from multiple areas are examined microscopically but, even then, sometimes the mites cannot be found.

Fortunately, scabies is relatively easy to treat, and there are a variety of products that will successfully kill the mites. Since the mites can't live in the environment for very long without feeding, a complete cure is usually possible within four to eight weeks.

Cheyletiellosis is caused by a relatively large mite, which sometimes can be seen even without a microscope. Often referred to as "walking dandruff," this also causes itching, but not usually as profound as with scabies.

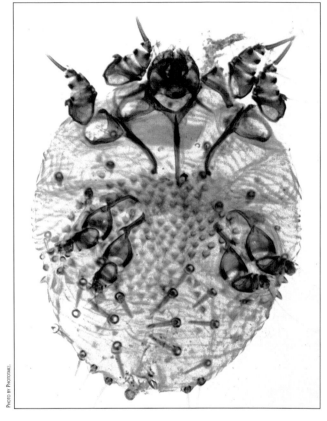

Photo by Photodisc.

Sarcoptes scabiei, commonly known as the "itch mite."

While *Cheyletiella* mites can survive somewhat longer in the environment than scabies mites, they too are relatively easy to treat, being responsive to not only the medications used to treat scabies but also often to flea-control products.

Otodectes cynotis is the canine ear mite and is one of the more common causes of mange, especially in young dogs in shelters or pet stores. That's because the mites are typically present in large numbers and are quickly spread to

Micrograph of a dog louse, *Heterodoxus spiniger*. Female lice attach their eggs to the hairs of the dog. As the eggs hatch, the larval lice bite and feed on the blood. Lice can also feed on dead skin and hair. This feeding activity can cause hair loss and skin problems.

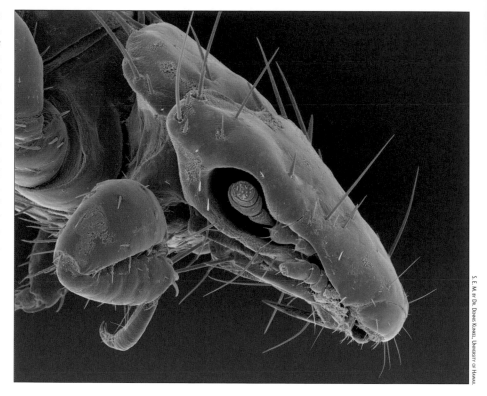

S. E. M. by Dr. Dennis Kunkel, University of Hawaii.

nearby animals. The mites rarely do much harm but can be difficult to eradicate if the treatment regimen is not comprehensive. While many try to treat the condition with ear drops only, this is the most common cause of treatment failure. Ear drops cause the mites to simply move out of the ears and as far away as possible (usually to the base of the tail) until the insecticide levels in the ears drop to an acceptable level—then it's back to business as usual! The successful treatment of ear mites requires treating all animals in the household with a systemic insecticide, such as selamectin, or a combination of miticidal ear drops combined with whole-body flea-control preparations.

Demodicosis, sometimes referred to as red mange, can be one of the most difficult forms of mange to treat. Part of the problem has to do with the fact that the mites live in the hair follicles and they are relatively well shielded from topical and systemic products. The main issue, however, is that demodectic mange typically results only when there is some underlying process interfering with the dog's immune system.

Since *Demodex* mites are

normal residents of the skin of mammals, including humans, there is usually a mite population explosion only when the immune system fails to keep the number of mites in check. In young animals, the immune deficit may be transient or may reflect an actual inherited immune problem. In older animals, demodicosis is usually seen only when there is another disease hampering the immune system, such as diabetes, cancer, thyroid problems or the use of immune-suppressing drugs. Accordingly, treatment involves not only trying to kill the mange mites but also discerning what is interfering with immune function and correcting it if possible.

Chiggers represent several different species of mite that don't parasitize dogs specifically, but do latch on to passersby and can cause irritation. The problem is most prevalent in wooded areas in the late summer and fall. Treatment is not difficult, as the mites do not complete their life cycle on dogs and are susceptible to a variety of miticidal products.

ILLUSTRATION BY PHOTOTAKE

Illustration of Demodex folliculoram.

MOSQUITOES

Mosquitoes have long been known to transmit a variety of diseases to people, as well as just being biting pests during warm weather. They also pose a real risk to pets. Not only do they carry deadly heartworms but recently there also has been much concern over their involvement with West Nile virus. While we can avoid heartworm with the use of preventive medications, there are no such preventives for West Nile virus. The only method of prevention in endemic areas is active mosquito control. Fortunately, most dogs that have been exposed to the virus only developed flu-like symptoms and, to date, there have not been the large number of reported deaths in canines as seen in some other species.

MOSQUITO REPELLENT

Low concentrations of DEET (less than 10%), found in many human mosquito repellents, have been safely used in dogs but, in these concentrations, probably give only about two hours of protection. DEET may be safe in these small concentrations, but since it is not licensed for use on dogs, there is no research proving its safety for dogs. Products containing permethrin give the longest-lasting protection, perhaps two to four weeks. As DEET is not licensed for use on dogs, and both DEET and permethrin can be quite toxic to cats, appropriate care should be exercised. Other products, such as those containing oil of citronella, also have some mosquito-repellent activity, but typically have a relatively short duration of action.

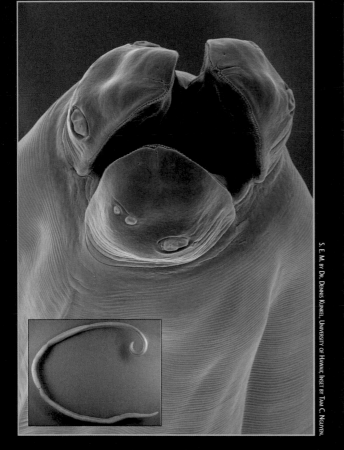

S. E. M. BY DR. DENNIS KUNKEL, UNIVERSITY OF HAWAII. INSET BY TAM C. NGUYEN.

ASCARID DANGERS

The most commonly encountered worms in dogs are roundworms known as ascarids. *Toxascaris leonine* and *Toxocara canis* are the two species that infect dogs. Subsisting in the dog's stomach and intestines, adult roundworms can grow to 7 inches in length and adult females can lay in excess of 200,000 eggs in a single day.

In humans, visceral larval migrans affects people who have ingested eggs of *Toxocara canis*, which frequently contaminates children's sandboxes, beaches and park grounds. The roundworms reside in the human's stomach and intestines, as they would in a dog's, but do not mature. Instead, they find their way to the liver, lungs and skin, or even to the heart or kidneys in severe cases. Deworming puppies is critical in preventing the infection in humans, and young children should never handle nursing pups who have not been dewormed.

The ascarid roundworm *Toxocara canis*, showing the mouth with three lips. INSET: Photomicrograph of the roundworm *Ascaris lumbricoides*.

INTERNAL PARASITES: WORMS

ASCARIDS

Ascarids are intestinal roundworms that rarely cause severe disease in dogs. Nonetheless, they are of major public health significance because they can be transferred to people. Sadly, it is children who are most commonly affected by the parasite, probably from inadvertently ingesting ascarid-contaminated soil. In fact, many yards and children's sandboxes contain appreciable numbers of ascarid eggs. So, while ascarids don't bite dogs or latch onto their intestines to suck blood, they do cause some nasty medical conditions in children and are best eradicated from our furry friends. Because pups can start passing ascarid eggs by three weeks of age, most parasite-control programs begin at two weeks of age and are repeated every two weeks until pups are eight weeks old. It is important to

HOOKED ON ANCYLOSTOMA

Adult dogs can become infected by the bloodsucking nematodes we commonly call hookworms via ingesting larvae from the ground or via the larvae penetrating the dog's skin. It is not uncommon for infected dogs to show no symptoms of hookworm infestation. Sometimes symptoms occur within ten days of exposure. These symptoms can include bloody diarrhea, anemia, loss of weight and general weakness. Dogs pass the hookworm eggs in their stools, which serves as the vet's method of identifying the infestation. The hookworm larvae can encyst themselves in the dog's tissues and be released when the dog is experiencing stress.

Caused by an *Ancylostoma* species whose common host is the dog, cutaneous larval migrans affects humans, causing itching and lumps and streaks beneath the surface of the skin.

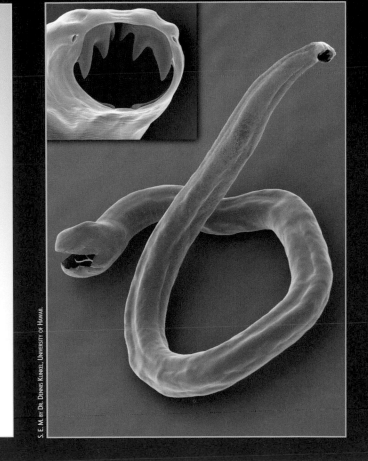

S. E. M. BY DR. DENNIS KUNKEL, UNIVERSITY OF HAWAII.

realize that bitches can pass ascarids to their pups even if they test negative prior to whelping. Accordingly, bitches are best treated at the same time as the pups.

HOOKWORMS
Unlike ascarids, hookworms do latch onto a dog's intestinal tract and can cause significant loss of blood and protein. Similar to ascarids, hookworms can be transmitted to humans, where they cause a condition known as cutaneous larval migrans. Dogs can become infected either by consuming the infective larvae or by the larvae's penetrating the skin directly. People most often get infected when they are lying on the ground (such as on a beach) and the larvae penetrate the skin. Yes, the larvae can penetrate through a beach blanket. Hookworms are typically susceptible to the same medications used to treat ascarids.

The hookworm *Ancylostoma caninum* infests the intestines of dogs. INSET: Note the row of hooks at the posterior end, used to anchor the worm to the intestinal wall.

WHIPWORMS

Whipworms latch onto the lower aspects of the dog's colon and can cause cramping and diarrhea. Eggs do not start to appear in the dog's feces until about three months after the dog was infected. This worm has a peculiar life cycle, which makes it more difficult to control than ascarids or hookworms. The good thing is that whipworms rarely are transferred to people.

Some of the medications used to treat ascarids and hookworms are also effective against whipworms, but, in general, a separate treatment protocol is needed. Since most of the medications are effective against the adults but not the eggs or larvae, treatment is typically repeated in three weeks, and then often in three

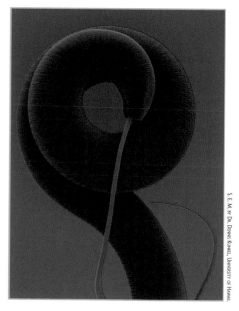

Adult whipworm, *Trichuris* sp., an intestinal parasite.

S. E. M. BY DR. DENNIS KUNKEL, UNIVERSITY OF HAWAII.

WORM-CONTROL GUIDELINES

- Practice sanitary habits with your dog and home.
- Clean up after your dog and don't let him sniff or eat other dogs' droppings.
- Control insects and fleas in the dog's environment. Fleas, lice, cockroaches, beetles, mice and rats can act as hosts for various worms.
- Prevent dogs from eating uncooked meat, raw poultry and dead animals.
- Keep dogs and children from playing in sand and soil.
- Kennel dogs on cement or gravel; avoid dirt runs.
- Administer heartworm preventives regularly.
- Have your vet examine your dog's stools at your annual visits.
- Select a boarding kennel carefully so as to avoid contamination from other dogs or an unsanitary environment.
- Prevent dogs from roaming. Obey local leash laws.

months as well. Unfortunately, since dogs don't develop resistance to whipworms, it is difficult to prevent them from getting reinfected if they visit soil contaminated with whipworm eggs.

TAPEWORMS

There are many different species of tapeworm that affect dogs, but *Dipylidium caninum* is probably the most common and is spread by fleas. Flea larvae feed on organic debris and tapeworm eggs in the environment and, when a dog chews at himself and manages to ingest fleas, he might get a dose of tapeworm at the same time. The tapeworm then develops further in the intestine of the dog.

The tapeworm itself, which is a parasitic flatworm that latches onto the intestinal wall, is composed of numerous segments. When the segments break off into the intestine (as proglottids), they may accumulate around the rectum, like grains of rice. While this tapeworm is disgusting in its behavior, it is not directly communicable to humans (although humans can also get infected by swallowing fleas).

A much more dangerous flatworm is *Echinococcus multilocularis*, which is typically found in foxes, coyotes and wolves. The eggs are passed in the feces and infect rodents, and, when dogs eat the rodents, the dogs can be infected by thousands of adult tapeworms. While the parasites don't cause many problems in dogs, this is considered the most lethal worm infection that people can get. Take appropriate precautions if you live in an area in which these tapeworms are found. Do not use mulch that may contain feces of dogs, cats or wildlife, and

discourage your pets from hunting wildlife. Treat these tapeworm infections aggressively in pets because if humans get infected, approximately half die.

HEARTWORMS

Heartworm disease is caused by the parasite *Dirofilaria immitis* and is seen in dogs around the world. A member of the roundworm group, it is spread between dogs by the bite of an infected mosquito. The mosquito injects infective larvae into the dog's skin with its bite, and these larvae develop under the skin for a period of time before making their way to the heart. There they develop into adults, which grow and create blockages of the heart, lungs and major blood vessels there. They also start producing offspring (microfilariae),

A dog tapeworm proglottid (body segment).

The dog tapeworm *Taenia pisiformis*.

S. E. M. BY DR. DENNIS KUNKEL, UNIVERSITY OF HAWAII.

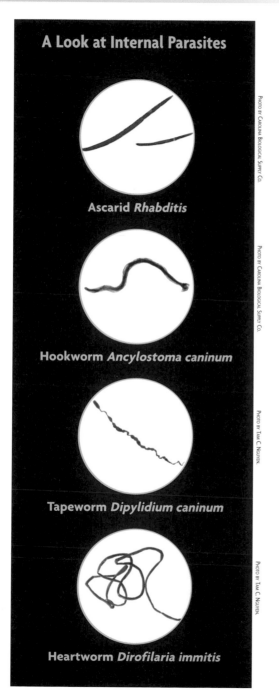

A Look at Internal Parasites

Ascarid *Rhabditis*

Hookworm *Ancylostoma caninum*

Tapeworm *Dipylidium caninum*

Heartworm *Dirofilaria immitis*

PHOTO BY CAROLINA BIOLOGICAL SUPPLY CO.

PHOTO BY CAROLINA BIOLOGICAL SUPPLY CO.

PHOTO BY TAM C. NGUYEN

PHOTO BY TAM C. NGUYEN

and these microfilariae circulate in the bloodstream, waiting to hitch a ride when the next mosquito bites. Once in the mosquito, the microfilariae develop into infective larvae and the entire process is repeated.

When dogs get infected with heartworm, over time they tend to develop symptoms associated with heart disease, such as coughing, exercise intolerance and potentially many other manifestations. Diagnosis is confirmed by either seeing the microfilariae themselves in blood samples or using immunologic tests (antigen testing) to identify the presence of adult heartworms. Since antigen tests measure the presence of adult heartworms and microfilarial tests measure offspring produced by adults, neither are positive until six to seven months after the initial infection. However, the beginning of damage can occur by fifth-stage larvae as early as three months after infection. Thus it is possible for dogs to be harboring problem-causing larvae for up to three months before either type of test would identify an infection.

The good news is that there are great protocols available for preventing heartworm in dogs. Testing is critical in the process, and it is important to understand the benefits as well as the limitations of such testing. All dogs six months of age or older that have not been on continuous heartworm-preventive medication should be

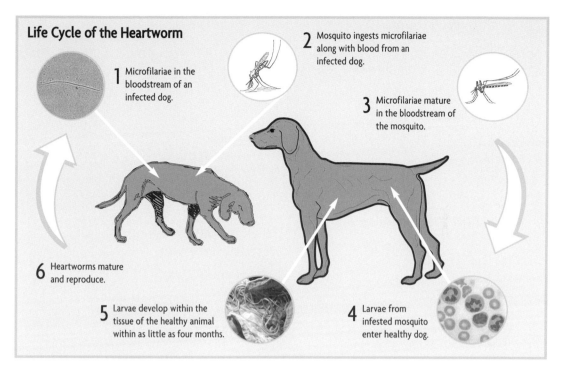

Life Cycle of the Heartworm

1 Microfilariae in the bloodstream of an infected dog.

2 Mosquito ingests microfilariae along with blood from an infected dog.

3 Microfilariae mature in the bloodstream of the mosquito.

6 Heartworms mature and reproduce.

5 Larvae develop within the tissue of the healthy animal within as little as four months.

4 Larvae from infested mosquito enter healthy dog.

screened with microfilarial or antigen tests. For dogs receiving preventive medication, periodic antigen testing helps assess the effectiveness of the preventives. The American Heartworm Society guidelines suggest that annual retesting may not be necessary when owners have absolutely provided continuous heartworm prevention. Retesting on a two- to three-year interval may be sufficient in these cases. However, your veterinarian will likely have specific guidelines under which heartworm preventives will be prescribed, and many prefer to err on the side of safety and retest annually.

It is indeed fortunate that heartworm is relatively easy to prevent because treatments can be as life-threatening as the disease itself. Treatment requires a two-step process that kills the adult heartworms first and then the microfilariae. Prevention is obviously preferable; this involves a once-monthly oral or topical treatment. The most common oral preventives include ivermectin (not suitable for some breeds), moxidectin and milbemycin oxime; the once-a-month topical drug selamectin provides heartworm protection in addition to flea, some types of tick and other parasite controls.

THE **ABC**s OF
Emergency Care

Abrasions
Clean wound with running water or 3% hydrogen peroxide. Pat dry with gauze and spray with antibiotic. Do not cover.

Animal Bites
Clean area with soap and saline solution or water. Apply pressure to any bleeding area. Apply antibiotic ointment. Identify animal and contact the vet.

Antifreeze Poisoning
Induce vomiting and take dog to the vet.

Bee Sting
Remove stinger and apply soothing lotion or cold compress; give antihistamine in proper dosage.

Bleeding
Apply pressure directly to wound with gauze or towel for five to ten minutes. If wound does not stop bleeding, wrap wound with gauze and adhesive tape.

Bloat/Gastric Torsion
Immediately take the dog to the vet or emergency clinic; phone from car. No time to waste.

Burns
Chemical: Bathe dog with water and pet shampoo. Rinse in saline solution. Apply antibiotic ointment.

Acid: Rinse with water. Apply one part baking soda, two parts water to affected area.

Alkali: Rinse with water. Apply one part vinegar, four parts water to affected area.

Electrical: Apply antibiotic ointment. Seek veterinary assistance immediately.

Choking
If the dog is on the verge of collapsing, wedge a solid object, such as the handle of a screwdriver, between molars on one side of the mouth to keep mouth open. Pull tongue out. Use long-nosed pliers or fingers to remove foreign object. Do not push the object down the dog's throat. For small or medium dogs, hold dog upside down by hind legs and shake firmly to dislodge foreign object.

Chlorine Ingestion
With clean water, rinse the mouth and eyes. Give the dog water to drink; contact the vet.

Constipation
Feed dog 2 tablespoons bran flakes with each meal. Encourage drinking water. Mix $1/4$-teaspoon mineral oil in dog's food.

Diarrhea
Withhold food for 12 to 24 hours. Feed dog anti-diarrheal with eyedropper. When feeding resumes, feed one part boiled hamburger, one part plain cooked rice, $1/4$- to $3/4$-cup four times daily. Contact vet if persists longer than 24 hours.

Dog Bite
Snip away hair around puncture wound; clean with 3% hydrogen peroxide; apply tincture of iodine. Identify biting dog and contact the vet. If wound appears deep, take the dog to the vet.

Frostbite
Wrap the dog in a heavy blanket. Warm affected area with a warm bath for ten minutes. Red color to skin will return with circulation; if tissues are pale after 20 minutes, contact the vet.

Use a portable, durable container large enough to contain all items.

Heat Stroke

Partially submerge the dog in cold water; if no response within ten minutes, contact the vet.

Hot Spots

Mix 2 packets Domeboro® with 2 cups water. Saturate cloth with mixture and apply to hot spots for 15 to 30 minutes. Apply antibiotic ointment. Repeat every six to eight hours.

Poisonous Plants

Wash affected area with soap and water. Cleanse with alcohol. For foxtail/grass, apply antibiotic ointment. Contact the vet if plant is ingested.

Rat Poison Ingestion

Induce vomiting. Keep dog calm, maintain dog's normal body temperature (use blanket or heating pad). Get to the vet for antidote.

Shock

Keep the dog calm and warm; call for veterinary assistance.

Snake Bite

If possible, bandage the area and apply pressure. If the area is not conducive to bandaging, use ice to control bleeding. Get immediate help from the vet.

Tick Removal

Apply flea and tick spray directly on tick. Wait one minute. Using tweezers or wearing plastic gloves, apply constant pull while grasping tick's body. Apply antibiotic ointment.

Vomiting

Restrict dog's water intake; offer a few ice cubes. Withhold food for next meal. Contact vet if vomiting persists longer than 24 hours.

DOG OWNER'S FIRST-AID KIT

- ❑ **Gauze bandages/swabs**
- ❑ **Adhesive and non-adhesive bandages**
- ❑ **Antibiotic powder**
- ❑ **Antiseptic wash**
- ❑ **Hydrogen peroxide 3%**
- ❑ **Antibiotic ointment**
- ❑ **Lubricating jelly**
- ❑ **Rectal thermometer**
- ❑ **Nylon muzzle**
- ❑ **Scissors and forceps**
- ❑ **Eyedropper**
- ❑ **Syringe**
- ❑ **Anti-bacterial/fungal solution**
- ❑ **Saline solution**
- ❑ **Antihistamine**
- ❑ **Cotton balls**
- ❑ **Nail clippers**
- ❑ **Screwdriver/pen knife**
- ❑ **Flashlight**
- ❑ **Emergency phone numbers**

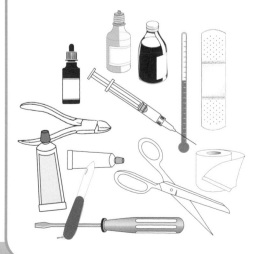

WHAT ARE THE SIGNS OF AGING?

By the time your dog has reached his senior years, you will know him very well, so the physical and behavioral changes that accompany aging should be noticeable to you. Humans and dogs share the most obvious physical sign of aging: gray hair! Graying often occurs first on the muzzle and face, around the eyes. Other telltale signs are the dog's overall decrease in activity. Your older dog might be more content to nap and rest, and he may not show the same old enthusiasm when it's time to play in the yard or go for a walk. Other physical signs include significant weight loss or gain; more labored movement; skin and coat problems, possibly hair loss; sight and/or hearing problems; changes in toileting habits, perhaps seeming "unhousebroken" at times; and tooth decay, bad breath or other mouth problems.

There are behavioral changes that go along with aging, too. There are numerous causes for behavioral changes. Sometimes a dog's apparent confusion results from a physical change like diminished sight or hearing. If his confusion causes him to be afraid, he may act aggressively or defensively. He may sleep more frequently because his daily walks, though shorter now, tire him out. He may begin to experience separation anxiety or, conversely, become less interested in petting and attention.

There also are clinical conditions that cause behavioral changes in older dogs. One such condition is known as canine cognitive dysfunction (familiarly known as "old-dog" syndrome). It can be frustrating for an owner whose dog is affected with cognitive dysfunction, as it can result in behavioral changes of all types, most seemingly unexplainable. Common changes include the dog's forgetting aspects of the daily routine, such as times to eat, go out for walks, relieve himself and the like. Along the same lines, you may take your dog out at the regular time for a potty trip and he may have no idea why he is there. Sometimes a placid dog will begin to show aggressive or possessive tendencies or, conversely, a hyperactive dog will start to "mellow out."

Disease also can be the cause of behavioral changes in senior dogs. Hormonal problems (Cushing's disease is common in older dogs), diabetes and thyroid disease can cause increased appetite, which can lead to aggression related to food guarding. It's better to be proactive with your senior dog, making more frequent trips to the vet if necessary and having bloodwork done to test for the diseases that can commonly befall older dogs.

This is not to say that, as dogs age, they all fall apart physically and become nasty in personality. The aforementioned changes are discussed to alert owners to the things that may happen as their dogs get older. Many hardy dogs remain active and alert well into old age; in fact, Briards often retain youthful behavior patterns of running, jumping and bouncing about until they are quite elderly. However, it can be frustrating and heartbreaking for owners to see their beloved dogs change

physically and temperamentally. Just know that it's the same Briard under there, and that he still loves you and appreciates your care, which he needs now more than ever.

HOW DO I CARE FOR MY AGING DOG?

Again, every dog is an individual in terms of aging. Your dog might advance in years and show no signs of slowing down. However, even if he shows no outward signs of aging, he should begin a senior-care program as determined by the vet. He may not show it, but he's not a pup anymore! By providing him with extra attention to his veterinary care at this age, you will be practicing good preventive medicine, ensuring that the rest of your dog's life will be as long, active, happy and healthy as possible. If you do notice indica-

Among the signs that your Briard has slowed down are his increased sleep periods and general decrease in activity.

tions of aging, such as graying and/or changes in sleeping, eating or toileting habits, this is a sign to set up a senior-care visit with your vet right away to make sure that these changes are not related to any health problems.

To start, senior dogs should visit the vet twice yearly for exams, routine tests and overall evaluations. Many vets have special screening programs especially for senior dogs that can include a thorough physical exam; blood test to determine complete blood count; serum biochemistry test, which screens for liver, kidney and blood problems as well as cancer; urinalysis; and dental exams. With these tests, it can be determined whether your dog has any health problems; the results also establish a baseline for your pet against which future test results can be compared.

In addition to these tests, your vet may suggest additional testing, including an EKG, tests for glaucoma and other problems of the eye, chest x-rays, screening for tumors, blood pressure test, test for thyroid function and screening for parasites and reassessment of his preventive program. Your vet also will ask you questions about your dog's diet and activity level, what you feed and the amounts that you feed. This information, along with his evaluation of the dog's overall condition, will enable him to suggest proper dietary changes, if needed.

This may seem like quite a work-up for your pet, but veterinarians advise that older dogs need more frequent attention so that any health problems can be detected as early as possible. Serious conditions like kidney disease, heart disease and cancer may not present outward symptoms, or the problem may go undetected if the symptoms are mistaken by owners as just part of the aging process.

Aside from the extra veterinary care, there is much you can do at home to keep your older dog in good condition. The dog's diet is an important factor. If your dog's appetite decreases, he will not be getting the nutrients he needs. He also will lose weight, which is unhealthy for a dog at a proper weight. Conversely, an older dog's metabolism is slower and he usually exercises less, but he should not be allowed to become obese. Obesity in an older dog is especially risky because extra pounds mean extra stress on the body, increasing his vulnerability to heart disease. Additionally, the extra pounds make it harder for the dog to move about.

You should discuss age-related feeding changes with your vet. For a dog who has lost interest in food, it may be suggested to try some different type s of food until you find something new that the dog likes. For an obese dog, a "light"-formula dog food or reducing food portions may be advised, along with exercise appropriate to his physical condition and energy level.

As for exercise, the senior dog should not be allowed to become a "couch potato" despite his old age. He may not be able to handle the morning run, long walks and vigorous games of fetch, but he still needs to get up and get moving. Keep up with your daily walks, but keep the distances shorter and let your dog set the pace. If he gets to the point where he's not up for walks, let him stroll around the yard. On the other hand, many dogs remain very active in their senior years, so base changes to the exercise

ACCIDENT ALERT!

You want to create a safe environment in which your dog can get around easily and comfortably, with no dangers. A dog that slips and falls in old age is much more prone to injury than an adult, making accident prevention even more important. Likewise, dogs are more prone to falls in old age, as they do not have the same balance and coordination that they once had. Throw rugs on hardwood floors are slippery and pose a risk; even a throw rug on a carpeted surface can be an obstacle for the senior dog. Consider putting down non-slip surfaces or confining your dog to carpeted rooms only.

program on your own individual dog and what he's capable of. Don't worry, your Briard will let you know when it's time to rest.

Keep up with your grooming routine as you always have. Be extra diligent about checking the skin and coat for problems. Older dogs can experience thinning coats as a normal aging process, but they can also lose hair as a result of medical problems. Some thinning is normal, but patches of baldness or the loss of significant amounts of hair is not.

Hopefully, you've been regular with brushing your dog's teeth throughout his life. Healthy teeth directly affect overall good health. We already know that bacteria from gum infections can enter the dog's body through the damaged gums and travel to the organs. At a stage in life when his organs don't function as well as they used to, you don't want anything to put additional strain on them. Clean teeth also contribute to a healthy immune system. Offering the dental-type chews in addition to toothbrushing can help, as they remove plaque and tartar as the dog chews.

Along with the same good care you've given him all of his life, pay a little extra attention to your dog in his senior years and keep up with twice-yearly trips to the vet. The sooner a problem is uncovered, the greater the chances of a full recovery.

Is dog showing in your blood? Are you excited by the idea of gaiting your handsome Briard around the ring to the thunderous applause of an enthusiastic audience? Are you certain that your beloved Briard is flawless? You are not alone! Every loving owner thinks that his dog has no faults, or too few to mention. No matter how many times an owner reads the breed standard, he cannot find any faults in his aristocratic companion dog. If this sounds like you, and if you are considering entering your Briard in a dog show, here are some basic questions to ask yourself:

- Did you purchase a "show-quality" puppy from the breeder?
- Is your puppy at least six months of age?
- Does the puppy exhibit correct show type for his breed?
- Does your puppy have any disqualifying faults?
- Is your Briard registered with the American Kennel Club?
- How much time do you have to devote to training, grooming, conditioning and exhibiting your dog?
- Do you understand the rules and regulations of a dog show?
- Do you have time to learn how to show your dog properly?
- Do you have the financial

resources to invest in showing your dog?
- Will you show the dog yourself or hire a professional handler?
- Do you have a vehicle that can accommodate your weekend trips to the dog shows?

Success in the show ring requires more than a pretty face, a waggy tail and a pocketful of liver. Even though dog shows can be exciting and enjoyable, the sport of conformation makes great demands on the exhibitors and the dogs. Winning exhibitors live for their dogs, devoting time and money to their dogs' presentation, conditioning and training. Very few novices, even those with good dogs, will find themselves in the winners' circle, though it does happen. Don't be disheartened, though. Every exhibitor began as a novice and worked his way up to the Group ring. It's the "working your way up" part that you must keep in mind.

Assuming that you have purchased a puppy of the correct type and quality for showing, let's begin to examine the world of showing and what's required to get started. Although the entry fee into a dog show is nominal, there are lots of other hidden costs involved with "finishing" your Briard, that is, making him a champion. Things like equipment, travel, training and conditioning all cost money. A more serious campaign will include fees for a professional handler, boarding, cross-country travel and advertising. Top-winning show dogs can represent a very considerable investment—over $100,000 has been spent in campaigning some dogs. (The investment can be less, of course, for owners who don't use professional handlers.)

Many owners, on the other hand, enter their "average" Briards in dog shows for the fun and enjoyment of it. Dog showing makes an absorbing hobby, with many rewards for dogs and owners alike. If you're having fun, meeting other people who share your interests and enjoying the overall experience, you likely will catch the "bug." Once the dog-show bug bites, its effects can last a lifetime; it's certainly much better than a deer tick! Soon you will be envisioning yourself in the center ring at the Westminster Kennel Club Dog Show in New York City, competing for the prestigious Best in Show cup. This magical dog show is televised annually from Madison Square Garden, and the victorious dog becomes a celebrity overnight.

Top-winning Ch. OhSayCanYouSee des Edennes de Colmel, handled by Jimmy Moses under judge Judy Harrington.

AKC CONFORMATION SHOWING

GETTING STARTED

Visiting a dog show as a spectator is a great place to start. Pick up the show catalog to find out what time your breed is being shown, who is judging the breed and in which ring the classes will be held. To start, Briards compete against other Briards, and the winner is selected as Best of Breed by the judge. This is the procedure for each breed. At a group show, all of the Best of Breed winners go on to compete for Group One in their respective groups. For example, all Best of Breed winners in a given group compete against each other; this is done for all seven groups. Finally, all seven group winners go head to head in the ring for the Best in Show award.

What most spectators don't understand is the basic idea of conformation. A dog show is often referred to as a "conformation" show. This means that the judge should decide how each dog stacks up (conforms) to the breed standard for his given breed: how well does this Briard conform to the ideal representative detailed in the standard? Ideally, this is what happens. In reality, however, this ideal often gets slighted as the judge compares Briard #1 to Briard #2. Again, the ideal is that each dog is judged based on his merits in comparison to his breed standard, not in comparison to the other dogs in the ring. It is easier for judges to compare dogs of the same breed to decide which they think is the better specimen; in the Group and Best in Show ring, however, it is very difficult to compare one breed to another, like apples to oranges. Thus the dog's conformation to the breed standard—not to mention advertising dollars and good handling—is essential to success in conformation shows. The dog described in the standard (the standard for each AKC breed is written and approved by the breed's national parent club and then submitted to the AKC for approval) is the perfect dog of that breed, and breeders keep their eye on the

---

FOR MORE INFORMATION...

For reliable up-to-date information about registration, dog shows and other canine competitions, contact one of the national registries by mail or via the Internet.

American Kennel Club
5580 Centerview Dr., Raleigh, NC 27606-3390
www.akc.org

United Kennel Club
100 E. Kilgore Road, Kalamazoo, MI 49002
www.ukcdogs.com

Canadian Kennel Club
89 Skyway Ave., Suite 100, Etobicoke, Ontario
M9W 6R4, Canada
www.ckc.ca

The Kennel Club
1-5 Clarges St., Piccadilly, London W1Y 8AB, UK
www.the-kennel-club.org.uk

standard when they choose which dogs to breed, hoping to get closer and closer to the ideal with each litter.

Another good first step for the novice is to join a dog club. You will be astonished by the many and different kinds of dog clubs in the country, with about 5,000 clubs holding events every year. Most clubs require that prospective new members present two letters of recommendation from existing members. Perhaps you've made some friends visiting a show held by a particular club and you would like to join that club. Dog clubs may specialize in a single breed, like a local or regional Briard club, or in a specific pursuit, such as obedience, tracking or hunting tests. There are all-breed clubs for all-dog enthusiasts; they sponsor special training days, seminars on topics like grooming or handling or lectures on breeding or canine genetics. There are also clubs that specialize in certain types of dogs, like herding dogs, hunting dogs, companion dogs, etc.

A parent club is the national organization, sanctioned by the AKC, which promotes and safeguards its breed in the country. The Briard Club of America was formed in 1928 and can be contacted on the Internet at www.briardclubofamerica.org. The parent club holds an annual national specialty show, usually in a different city each year, in which

many of the country's top dogs, handlers and breeders gather to compete. At a specialty show, only members of a single breed are invited to participate. There are also group specialties, in which all members of a group are invited. For more information about dog clubs in your area, contact the AKC at www.akc.org on the Internet or write them at their Raleigh, NC address.

How Shows Are Organized

Three kinds of conformation shows are offered by the AKC. There is the all-breed show, in which all AKC-recognized breeds can compete; the specialty show, which is for one breed only and usually sponsored by the breed's parent club and the group show, for all breeds in one of the AKC's seven groups. The Briard

Attending an outdoor all-breed or specialty show can be an exciting experience for newcomers. You will learn much about how shows work and also more about the Briard.

BOB at the Briard Club of America specialty in 2003, Ch. Déjà Vu Rhymin' Simon, handled by Greg Strong under judge Denny Kodner.

competes in the Herding Group.

For a dog to become an AKC champion of record, the dog must earn 15 points at shows. The points must be awarded by at least three different judges and must include two "majors" under different judges. A "major" is a three-, four- or five-point win, and the number of points per win is determined by the number of dogs competing in the show on that day. (Dogs that are absent or are excused are not counted.) The number of points that are awarded varies from breed to breed. More dogs are needed to attain a major in more popular breeds, and fewer dogs are needed in less popular breeds. Yearly, the AKC evaluates the number of dogs in competition in each division (there are 14 divisions in all, based

on geography) and may or may not change the numbers of dogs required for each number of points. For example, a major in Division 2 (Delaware, New Jersey and Pennsylvania) recently required 17 dogs or 16 bitches for a three-point major, 29 dogs or 27 bitches for a four-point major and 51 dogs or 46 bitches for a five-point major. The Briard attracts numerically proportionate representation at all-breed shows.

Only one dog and one bitch of each breed can win points at a given show. There are no "co-ed" classes except for champions of record. Dogs and bitches do not compete against each other until they are champions. Dogs that are not champions (referred to as "class dogs") compete in one of five classes. The class in which a dog is entered depends on age and previous show wins. First there is the Puppy Class (sometimes divided further into classes for 6- to 9-month-olds and 9- to 12-month-olds); next is the Novice Class (for dogs that have no points toward their championship and whose only first-place wins have come in the Puppy Class or the Novice Class, the latter class limited to three first places); then there is the American-bred Class (for dogs bred in the US); the Bred-by-Exhibitor Class (for dogs handled by their breeders or by immediate family members of their breeders); and the Open Class (for any non-champions). Any dog may enter the Open Class, regardless of age or win history, but to be competitive the dog should be older and have ring experience.

The judge at the show begins judging the male dogs in the Puppy Class(es) and proceeds through the other classes. The judge awards first through fourth place in each class. The first-place winners of each class then compete with one another in the Winners Class to determine Winners Dog. The judge then starts over with the bitches, beginning with the Puppy Class(es) and proceeding up to the Winners Class to award Winners Bitch, just as he did with the dogs. A Reserve

Winners Dog and Reserve Winners Bitch are also selected; they could be awarded the points in the case of a disqualification.

The Winners Dog and Winners Bitch are the two that are awarded the points for their breed. They then go on to compete with any champions of record (often called "specials") of their breed that are entered in the show. The champions may be dogs or bitches; in this class, all are shown together. The judge reviews the Winners Dog and Winners Bitch along with all of the champions to select the Best of Breed winner. The Best of Winners is selected between the Winners Dog

Ch. Déjà Vu Runaround Sue, shown by Larry Cornelius under judge Judith Goodin.

PHOTO SUSAN B. LENNAH.

and Winners Bitch; if one of these two is selected Best of Breed as well, he or she is automatically determined Best of Winners. Lastly, the judge selects Best of Opposite Sex to the Best of Breed winner. The Best of Breed winner then goes on to the group competition.

At a group or all-breed show, the Best of Breed winners from each breed are divided into their respective groups to compete against one

another for Group One through Group Four. Group One (first place) is awarded to the dog that best lives up to the ideal for his breed as described in the standard. A group judge, therefore, must have a thorough working knowledge of many breed standards. After placements have been made in each group, the seven Group One winners (from the Sporting Group, Toy Group, Hound Group, etc.)

compete against each other for the top honor, Best in Show.

There are different ways to find out about dog shows in your area. The American Kennel Club's monthly magazine, the *American Kennel Gazette* is accompanied by, the *Events Calendar*; this magazine is available through subscription. You can also look on the AKC's and your parent club's websites for information and check the event listings in your local newspaper.

Your Briard must be six months of age or older and registered with the AKC in order to be entered in AKC-sanctioned shows in which there are classes for the Briard. Your Briard also must not possess any disqualifying faults and must be sexually intact. The reason for the latter is simple: dog shows are the proving grounds to determine which dogs and bitches are worthy of being bred. If they cannot be bred, that defeats the purpose! On that note, only dogs that have achieved championships, thus proving their excellent quality, should be bred. If you have spayed or neutered your dog, however, there are many AKC events other than conformation, such as obedience trials, agility trials and the Canine Good Citizen® Program, in which you and your Briard can participate.

OTHER TYPES OF COMPETITION

In addition to conformation shows, the AKC holds a variety of other competitive events. Obedience trials, agility trials and tracking trials are open to all breeds, while hunting tests, field trials, lure coursing, herding tests and trials, earthdog tests and coonhound events are limited to specific breeds or groups of breeds. The Junior Showmanship program is offered to aspiring young handlers and their dogs, and the Canine Good Citizen® Program is an all-around good-behavior test open to all dogs, pure-bred and mixed.

The pipe tunnel is a favorite obstacle at agility trials.

Briards are capable of high levels of success in many types of performance events. This dog retrieves a dumbbell in an obedience competition.

Briards are capable of high levels of success in many types of performance events. This dog retrieves a dumbbell in an obedience competition.

OBEDIENCE TRIALS

Mrs. Helen Whitehouse Walker, a Standard Poodle fancier, can be credited with introducing obedience trials to the United States. In the 1930s she designed a series of exercises based on those of the Associated Sheep, Police, Army Dog Society of Great Britain. These exercises were intended to evaluate the working relationship between dog and owner. Since those early days of the sport in the US, obedience trials have grown more and more popular, and now more than 2,000 trials each year attract over 100,000 dogs and their owners.

Any dog registered with the AKC, regardless of neutering or other disqualifications that would preclude entry in conformation competition, can participate in obedience trials.

There are three levels of difficulty in obedience competition. The first (and easiest) level is the Novice, in which dogs can earn the Companion Dog (CD) title. The intermediate level is the Open level, in which the Companion Dog Excellent (CDX) title is awarded. The advanced level is the Utility level, in which dogs compete for the Utility Dog (UD) title. Classes at each level are further divided into "A" and "B," with "A" for beginners and "B" for those with more experience. In order to win a title at a given level, a dog must earn three "legs." A "leg" is accomplished when a dog scores 170 or higher (200 is a perfect score). The scoring system gets a little trickier when you understand that a dog must score more than 50% of the points available for each exercise in order to actually earn the points. Available points for each exercise range between 20 and 40.

A dog must complete different exercises at each level of obedience. The Novice exercises are the easiest, with the Open and finally the Utility levels progressing in difficulty. Examples of Novice exercises are on- and off-lead heeling, a figure-8 pattern, performing a recall (or come), long sit and long down and standing for examination. In the Open level, the Novice-level exercises are required again, but this time without a leash and for longer durations. In addition, the dog must clear a broad jump, retrieve over a jump and drop on recall. In the Utility level, the exercises are quite difficult, including executing basic commands based on hand signals, following a complex heeling pattern, locating articles based on scent discrimination and completing jumps at the handler's direction.

Once he's earned the UD title, a dog can go on to win the prestigious title of Utility Dog Excellent (UDX) by winning "legs" in ten shows. Additionally, Utility Dogs who win "legs" in Open B and Utility B earn points toward the lofty title of Obedience Trial Champion (OTCh.). Established in 1977 by the AKC, this title requires a dog to earn 100 points as well as three first places in a combination of Open B and Utility B classes under three different judges. The "brass ring" of obedience competition is the AKC's National Obedience Invitational. This is an exclusive competition for only the cream of the obedience crop. In order to qualify for the invitational, a dog must be ranked in either the top 25 all-breeds in obedience or in the top 3 for his breed in obedience. The title at stake here is that of National Obedience Champion (NOC).

AGILITY TRIALS

Agility trials became sanctioned by the AKC in August 1994, when the first licensed agility trials were held. Since that time, agility certainly has grown in popularity by leaps and bounds, literally! The AKC allows all registered breeds (including Miscellaneous Class breeds) to participate, providing the dog is 12 months of age or older. Agility is designed so that the handler demonstrates how well the dog can work at his side. The handler directs his dog through, over, under and around an obstacle course that includes jumps, tires, the dog walk, weave poles, pipe tunnels, collapsed tunnels and more. While working his way through the course, the dog must keep one eye and ear on the handler and the rest of his body on the course. The handler runs along with the dog, giving verbal and hand signals to guide the dog through the course.

The first organization to promote agility trials in the US was the United States Dog Agility Association, Inc. (USDAA). Established in 1986, the USDAA sparked the formation of many member clubs around the country. To participate in USDAA trials, dogs must be at least 18 months of age.

Agility trials are a great way to keep your dog active, and they will keep you running, too! You should join a local agility club to learn more about the sport. These clubs offer sessions in which you can introduce your dog to the various obstacles as well as training classes to prepare him for competition. In no time, your dog will be climbing A-frames, crossing the dog walk and flying over hurdles, all with you right beside him. Your heart will leap every time your dog jumps through the hoop.

HERDING EVENTS

The first recorded sheepdog trial was held in Wales in the late 19th century; since then, the popularity of herding events has grown around the world. The AKC began offering herding events in 1989, and participation is open to all breeds in the Herding Group as well as Rottweilers and Samoyeds. These events are designed to evaluate the dogs' herding instincts, and the aim is to develop those innate skills and show that herding dogs today can still perform the functions for which they were originally intended, whether or not they are actually used in working capacities. Herding events are designed to simulate farm situations and are held on two levels: tests and trials.

AKC herding tests are more basic and are scored on a pass/fail system, meaning that dogs do not compete against each other to earn titles. Titles at this level are the most basic Herding Tested (HT) and the more difficult Pre-Trial Tested (PT). In addition, there is a non-competitive certification program, Herding Instinct Tested, which gives you a chance to evaluate the potential that your dog may have for herding. If your dog successfully passes this test, he receives a Herding Instinct Certificate, which makes him eligible to enter herding trials.

Simulating actual farm work, a herding trial requires the dog to pen the livestock, in this case sheep.

The more challenging herding trial level is competitive and requires more training and experience. There are three different courses (A, B and C, each with a different type of farm situation) with different types of livestock (cattle, sheep or ducks). There are three titles available on each course, Herding Started, Herding Intermediate and Herding Advanced, with each level being progressively more difficult. Handlers can choose the type of course and type of livestock for their dogs based on the breed's typical use. Once a Herding Advanced title has been earned on a course, the dog can then begin to strive for the Herding Champion title.

In addition to events held by the AKC, breed clubs often hold herding events for these breeds. Other specialty organizations hold trials that are open to all herding breeds; the way these events are structured and the titles that are awarded differ from those of the AKC. For example, the American Herding Breed Association (AHBA) allows any breed with herding in its ancestry to participate, as well as allowing mixed-breed herding dogs. To pass the Herding Instinct Test,

Taking a break from normal routine, both herder and herdee seem to be distracted by the same outside influence.

the handler works with the dog at the shepherd's direction while the shepherd evaluates the dog's willingness to approach, move and round up the sheep while at the same time following the instructions of his handler.

At the competition level in AHBA events, dogs work with their handlers to move sheep up and down the field, through gates and into a pen, and also to hold the sheep without a pen, all while being timed. This is an amazing sight to see! A good dog working with the shepherd has to be the ultimate man-dog interaction. Rare breeds were often traditionally used for herding and, fortunately, the AHBA is more than happy to have rare breeds participate. Club members and spectators love to welcome some of these wonderful dogs that they have only read about but never seen.

A or agouti series 29
Acetaminophen toxicity 73
Activities 109
Activity level 23
—of senior dog 141, 143
Adenovirus 116, 118
Adult
—adoption 92
—feeding 76
—health 113
—training 90, 92
Aggression 68, 92, 119
Agility trials 109, 151, 153
Aging 113, 140
Airedale Terrier **31**
All-breed show 150
Alpha role 34
American Heartworm Society
  137
American Herding Breed
  Association 155
American Kennel Club 18, 34,
  144, 146, 147, 151
—competitive events 151-155
—conformation showing 146
—first Briard registered 18
—standard 34, 38-47
American Kennel Gazette 151
American Veterinary Medical
  Association 66
American-bred Class 148
Anatolian Shepherd Dog **11**
Ancylostoma caninum **133**, **136**
Anemia 78
Annual vet exams 113
Antifreeze 67
Appetite loss 112
Ascarid **132**, 133
Ascaris lumbricoides **132**
Attention 99, 101, 106
B or black series 26
Balkans 9, 13
Bathing 23, 83-84
Bearded Collie 14
Bearded sheepdogs 13
Beardsanbrow's Utopia **20**
Beauceron 9, **14**, 15-16, 31, 40,
  48-49
Bedding 60, 68, 95
Bedford, Professor Peter 120
Behavior
—of senior dog 140
—patterns 10
Bellhaven kennel 19
Bernese Mountain Dog 13
Best in Show 146, 151
Best of Breed 146, 149-150
—Westminster winners 18-22
Best of Opposite Sex 150
Best of Winners 149
Bloat 24, 76, 79, 81, 114
Blue coat color 33
Body language 92, 96, 103
Bones 61
Bordetella bronchiseptica 117,
  118
Borrelia burgdorferi 118
Borreliosis 117
Boulet Griffon 37
Boulet, Monsieur 37
Bowls 58
—elevated 114
Bred-by-Exhibitor Class 148

Breeder 53, 146
—selection 55-56, 111
Briard Club of America 16, 18,
  54
Britain 15-17, 36
Brushing 82-83
Carpathian Basin 14
C'est Bonheur Woodbine Tinsel
  8, 20
Canadian Kennel Club 146
Cancer 119
Canine cough 118
Canine development schedule
  93
Canine Good Citizen® Program
  151
Car travel 53
Central progressive retinal atro-
  phy 24, 120
Challenge Certificate 17
—first winner 15
Champion 148
—first American 15, 18
—first British 17
Chew toys 60-62, 69, 73, 95-96
Chewing 60-62, 69, 72
Cheyletiella mite **129**
Chien d'Aubrey 10
Chiggers 131
Children 23, 26, 68, 70, 72, 92
China 11
Chocolate 74
Class dogs 148
Classes at shows 148
Classification of dogs 9-10
Clicker training 107
Club Français du Chien du
  Berger 36
Clubs 147
Coat 23, 48, 82
—of senior dog 143
—show 83
Cognitive dysfunction 114
Collars 62, 63, 100
Color 15, 31, 34
—allowed by AKC 34
—genetics 24-34
Come 102, 105-106
Commands 52, 101-108
Commitment of ownership 23-
  24, 52-53, 56-58
Companion Dog 152
Competitive events 151-155
Conformation shows 145-151
—classes at 148
—getting started 146
—requirements for 151
Consistency 71, 95, 98
Core vaccines 117
Coronavirus 113, 118
Corrections 99
Crate 58-60, 68, 95
—pads 60
—training 94-98
Crufts 17
Crying 69, 95
Ctenocephalides canis **124**
D or dilution series 27
Dangers in the home 64, 67
Dauphine de Montjoye 18
DEET 131
Déjà Vu Briards 20
Déjà Vu Every Little Breeze 21

Déjà Vu Four Leaf Clover **8**
Déjà Vu House On Fire 21
Déjà Vu In Like Flynn **20**, 21
Déjà Vu Nine to Five 21
Déjà Vu Purple People Eater **21**
Déjà Vu Rhymin' Simon **148**
Déjà Vu Ruffles Have Ridges 21
Déjà Vu Runaround Sue **149**
Déjà Vu Woodbine Cheap
  Thrills **8**
Demodex mite **131**
Demodicosis 130-131
Dental care 50, 112, 114
—of senior dog 143
Desamee kennel 17
Desamee Leon Hubert 17
Desamee Mitzi Moffat 17
Desamee Tripot de Vasouy 15, **17**
Dewclaws 38, 48
Deworming 54
Diet 74-80
—adult 76
—puppy 74
—senior 77, 142-143
—sheet 56
Dilatation 79
Dipylidium caninum 134, **136**
Dirofilaria immitis 135, **136**, **137**
Discipline 72, 98
Distemper 116, 117, 118
Documentation 55-56
Dodge, Mrs. Geraldine
  Rockefeller 19
Dog types 9
Domestication of dogs 9-10
Dominance 102
Double dewclaws 38, 48
Down 96, 103
Down/stay 105
Dry baths 84
Drying 83
Duval, Mademoiselle Raoul 18
E or extension of black into the
  coat series 32
Ears 50, 83
—cleaning 86
—mite infestation 86, 129-130
Echinococcus multilocularis
  135
Emergency care 79, 138-139
Enchanted Briards 22, 34
Energy level 23
Enthusiasm 23
Establishing leadership 34, 70,
  91, 98
Estrela Mountain Dog 13
Estrus 119
European sheepdogs 9, 13-14
Events Calendar 151
Exercise 79, 81
—for senior dog 143
—pen 94
Expenses of ownership 54
External parasites 124-131
Eyes
—care of 83, 87
—color 50
—diseases 24, 56, 120-123
Family meeting the puppy 67
Farming 10, 13
Fear 68
—period 70
Feeding 74-80, 114

Feet 83
Fenced yard 66, 81
Field trials 151
First aid 79, 138-139
First night in new home 68
Fleas **124**, 125, **126**
Food 74-80, 95
—bowls 58
—loss of interest in 112
—poisonous to dogs 74, 78
—rewards 91, 98, 108-109
—types 78
France 10, 14, 36
French Club for Sheepdogs 37
French imports 19
French Stud Book 15
G or graying series 32
Gastric torsion 24, 76, 79, 81,
  114
Gastroplexy 79
Genetic testing 111
Genetics of color 24-34
Giardia 118
Grapes 74
Great Pyrenees 13
Greece 13
Grooming 23, 82-88
Group competition 146, 150
Group wins 19-22
Growth 52, 81, 93
Guard dog 23
Gum disease 112
Handler 144
Head structure 48
Health
—adult 113
—benefits of dog ownership 25
—insurance for pets 67, 116
—journal 67
—problems 24, 56, 120-123
—puppy 56, 111
—senior dog 114, 142
Heart disease 114
Heartworm 112, 135, **136**, **137**
Heat cycle 119
Heel 107-108
Hepatitis 116, 117, 118
Herding events 109, 151, 154
Herding Group 19-21
Herding history 21
Herding titles 154-155
Herdsman, The 22
Hereditary problems 24, 120-
  123
Heterodoxus spiniger **130**
Himalayas 11
Hip dysplasia 21, 24, 56, 121
*History of Herding Briards in
  the USA, A* 22
Holidays 53
Homemade toys 62
Hookworm **133**, **136**
Hoppin, Miss Frances 18
House-training 58, 92-98, 100
Hubert 17
Hungary 14
Hypothyroidism 24, 56
Identification 88
Ilch, Mrs. Florence B. 19
Independent thinking 23
Infectious diseases 117
Insurance 64, 116
Internal parasites 132-137

Intuition 26
Iraq 11
Ireland 16-17
Ixodes dammini **127-128**
Jefferson, Thomas 22
Jennie d'el Pastre 19, 21
Judges 148-149
Jumping up 96
Junior Showmanship 151
Kennel Club, The 146
Kidney problems 114
Komondor **13**, 14
Kyi Apso 14
Lafayette, Marquis de 22
Leash 62, 100
—pulling on 108
Leave it 102
Leptospirosis 117, 118
Lifespan 113
Livestock guardians 9-10, 13, 22
Louse **130**
Lyme disease 117
Macaire, Richard de 10
Majors 148
Mammary cancer 119
Maudie 17
Mendel, Gregor 28
Microchip 88
Miller, Terry 20
Mioritic Sheepdog 14
Miscellaneous Class 153
Mites **129**, 130, **131**
Montdidier, Sir Aubrey de 10
Morley, Gaby 32
Mosquitoes **131**, 135, 137
Mountain Dogs 13
Mounting 119
Multi-dog household 81
Nail clipping 85
Name 101, 107
Nanie de la Haute Tour 19-20
National Obedience Champion 153
Near East 11, 13
Neolithic Age 11, 13
Neutering 112, 117-120, 151
New Stone Age 11, 13
Niobe Chez Phydeaux 19
Nipping 72
Non-core vaccines 117
North American Rassemblement 16
Nougaret, Jean 123
Novice Class 148
Nuts 74
Obedience
—classes 109
—Trial Champion 153
—trials 104, 109, 152
Obesity 76, 77, 142
Off 96
OhSayCanYouSee des Edennes de Colmel **145**
Okay 103, 108
Onions 78
Open Class 148
Orthopedic Foundation for Animals 21
Other dogs 81, 119
Other pets 92
Otodectes cynotis 139
Outdoor safety 66, 81
Ovariohysterectomy 119
Ownership 23-24, 52-53, 56-58
—expenses of 54
—health benefits of 25

Pack animals 71
Panthere del Pastre **18**
Paper-training 94, 96
Parainfluenza 117
Parasites
—control 112
—external 120, 124-131
—internal 132-137
Parent club 147, 151
Parvovirus 116, 117, 118
Patience 92, 98
Pedigree 56
Personality 23, 34
Phillips System of Top Dogs 19, 21
Phydeaux Briards 21
Phydeaux Polly Poulet **19**
Phydeaux Quelques 19
Phydeaux Quoin de Cuivre 19-20
Phydeaux What's Happening 20
Picardy Sheepdog 14-15
Plants 113
Playtime 105
Point systems for show dogs 21
Poisons 66-67, 73, 74, 78, 113
Popularity 16
Positive reinforcement 68, 98-99, 101, 107
Praise 91, 98, 108-109
Preventive care 111, 113-114
Proglottid **135**
Progressive retinal atrophy 24, 120
Prostate problems 119
Pulling on leash 108
Punishment 98-99
Puppy
—appearance 54
—development 52
—diet 74
—establishing leadership 34, 70, 91, 98
—exercise 81
—feeding 56, 74
—first car ride 53
—first night in new home 68
—grooming 82
—health 54, 56, 111
—kindergarten training class 100
—meeting the family 67
—needs 94
—personality 56, 111
—selection 53-57, 111
—show quality 57, 144
—socialization 68, 69-71
—supplies for 58
—teething 69, 73
—temperament 57, 59
—training 68, 71, 90, 98
Puppy Class 148
Puppy-proofing 52
Pyrenean Mountain Dog 13
Pyrenean Sheepdog 14, **15**
Pythias Chez Phydeaux 19
Rabies 116, 117, 118
Racing 109
Raisins 74
Rassemblement 16
Rawhide 61
Regent de la Pommeraie 15, 18
Registration 56
Reserve Winners 149
Retinal pigment epithelial dystrophy 24, 120

Rewards 91, 98, 108-109
Rhabditis **136**
Roaming 119
Romania 13, 14
Rope toys 62
Roundworm **132**, 133, **136**
Routine 95
RPED 24, 120
Safety 52-53, 59, 65-67, 73, 78, 94, 96, 102, 105
—with toys 60-62
Sarcoptes scabiei **129**
Scabies 129
Scent attraction 97
Schedule 95, 97
Schlintz, Irene Castle Khatoonian 19
Scissors bite 50
Scotland 9, 14
Seiger show 16
Selecting a puppy 53-57, 111
Sendero's Lillian **150**
Senior dog 113
—activity level 141, 143
—behavioral changes 140
—dental care 143
—diet 77, 142-143
—exercise 143
—signs of aging 140
—veterinary care 114-115, 142
Separation of Briard and Beauceron 14-15
Shannon kennels 17
Sheepdogs 9, 13-14, 23
Shopping for puppy needs 58
Show quality 57, 144
Shows 54
—conformation 145-151
—costs of 144
—early 14, 36-37
—first classes 17
—in different countries 16
—types of 147
Sighthounds 10, **11**
Sit 101
Sit/stay 104
Smooth-faced Pyrenean Sheepdog 14
Snipe 44
Socialization 68, 69-71, 101, 112
Soft toys 61
South Russian Ovcharka 14
Soviet Union 14
Spaying 112, 117-120, 151
Specials 149
Specialty show 147
Spot bath 84
Standard 146
—AKC 34, 38-47
—comments on 47-50
—early 36
Stationary night blindness 24, 122
Stay 104, 108
Stomach stapling 79
Stonehills I'm Henri 19
Strangers 23
Stress 102
Supervision 73, 96
Surgery 119
Taenia pisiformis **135**
Tail 38, 48
Tapeworm 134, **135**, **136**
Tattoo 89
Teeth 50, 112, 114
Teething 69, 73

Temperament 23, 54, 57, 59, 111
Testicular cancer 119
Therapy dog 109
Tibet 11, 14
Tibetan Mastiff 11, 14
Tick-borne diseases 127
Ticks **127-128**
Timing 97-98, 106
Tingley, Mary Lou 21
Tomlin, Mike and Nancy 16-17
Toxascaris leonine 132
Toxins 66-67, 73, 74, 78
—plants 113
Toxocara canis **132**
Toys 60-62, 69, 73, 95-96
Tracking 109, 151
Training 23, 52
—basic principles of 90, 98, 102
—clicker 107
—commands 101-108
—consistent 71, 95, 98
—early 71
—importance of timing 97, 106
—potty 92-98
—puppy 68, 98
—safety tips 102
Transhumance 23
Travel 59
Traveling 53
Treats 68, 76, 91, 98
—weaning off in training 108-109
Trichuris sp. **134**
Tricks 109
Trimming 83
Trueman, Mr. and Mrs. 17
Turgis, Mademoiselle 15
Turkey 11, 13
Type 144
Umbilical hernias 54
United Kennel Club 146
United States 15-16, 18-22
—Dog Agility Association 153
Urine marking 119
Utility Dog 152
Utility Dog Excellent 153
Vaccinations 54, 66-67, 70, 112, 114, 116, 117
Veterinarian 61-62, 66-67, 112-114
Veterinary insurance 64, 116
Veterinary specialties 115
Visiting the litter 56
Volvulus 79
Von Willebrand's disease 56
Wait 102
Walker, Mrs. Helen Whitehouse 152
Watchdog 22
Water 79-80, 95
—bowls 58
Weir-Anderson, Mary 22, 34
Westminster Kennel Club 145
—Best of Breed winners 18-22
—first Group winner 20
West Nile virus 121
Whelan, Mrs. Albert 18
Whining 69, 95
Whipworm **134**
Winners Class 149
Working Group 19-20
World Wars 14-16, 18
Worm control 134
Yard 66, 81
Yugoslavia 13

My Briard

PUT YOUR PUPPY'S FIRST PICTURE HERE

Dog's Name _____

Date _____ Photographer _____